The
Troublemaker's Teaparty

The

Troublemaker's Teaparty

A Manual for Effective Citizen Action

Charles Dobson

NEW SOCIETY PUBLISHERS

Cataloguing in Publication Data:

A catalog record for this publication is available from the National Library of Canada.

Printed in Canada by Transcontinental Printing.

New Society Publishers acknowledges the support of the Government of Canada through the Book Publishing Industry Development Program (BPIDP) for our publishing activities.

Paperback ISBN: 0-86571-489-4

Inquiries regarding requests to reprint all or part of *The Troublemaker's Teaparty* should be addressed to New Society Publishers at the address below.

To order directly from the publishers, please add $4.50 shipping to the price of the first copy, and $1.00 for each additional copy (plus GST in Canada). Send check or money order to:

New Society Publishers

P.O. Box 189, Gabriola Island, BC V0R 1X0, Canada

1-800-567-6772

New Society Publishers' mission is to publish books that contribute in fundamental ways to building an ecologically sustainable and just society, and to do so with the least possible impact on the environment, in a manner that models this vision. We are committed to doing this not just through education, but through action. We are acting on our commitment to the world's remaining ancient forests by phasing out our paper supply from ancient forests worldwide. This book is one step towards ending global deforestation and climate change. It is printed on acid-free paper that is **100% old growth forest-free** (100% post-consumer recycled), processed chlorine free, and printed with vegetable based, low VOC inks. For further information, or to browse our full list of books and purchase securely, visit our website at: www.newsociety.com

NEW SOCIETY PUBLISHSERS   www.newsociety.com

Contents

Before You Begin
Beginning
Forming a Core Group
Getting to Know One Another
Getting More People
Door-knocking
Block-by-Block Organizing
Organizing Around an Issue
Keeping People Involved
Leading
Meeting
Information Sharing
Fundraising

Dialogue
Deep Community
Wrangling Reduction
Mediation and Conflict Resolution
Group Structure

Real Projects Make Messy Diagrams
Researching a Project
Planning a Project
Carrying Out a Project
Publicizing a project
Evaluating a project

Community Protection
Environmental Projects
Community Image-making
Celebrations

Surveys, Petitions, Research
Media Advisories / News Releases
Newspaper Editorial Pages
Video News Releases
Press Conferences
Ads That Become News
Cable TV Production
Radio
Preparing for Interviews
Narrowcasting

Hold On
Rules for Radicals
Citizen Investigations
Web Action
Direct Action
Extreme Versions of Direct Action

Appendices

Preface

THIS BOOK IS AN OUTGROWTH of a 1995 project to provide a grass-roots organizing guide for the citizens of Vancouver, British Columbia. *The Citizen's Handbook: A Guide to Building Community in Vancouver* arose out of a call for more meaningful citizen participation from many quarters. Many ordinary citizens wanted to know how they could effect changes in their neighborhoods by working with local government.

Experts were also calling for more citizen involvement. Around the same time five local task force reports appeared covering a range of issues – health care; climate change; child protection; safety; urban landscape; family services; and the environment and the economy. Despite the range of issues, all the reports came to the same conclusion: To make real progress on large-scale social problems we need far more citizen participation; more people involved in public life; more people willing to step beyond the bounds of their private property and the private world of friends and family. In other words, we need strong democracy; deep, broad, citizen involvement in public interest issues as a regular – if small – part of everyday life.

But there was a problem. There was a great gap between what the task force reports called for and what was actually happening. In Vancouver, only a handful of people were involved in local issues on a regular basis. The city did public participation projects when it felt necessary, but these always involved short-term, "hit and run" participation. In most cases, it was done to garner support for initiatives devised by bureaucrats. While city bureaucrats claimed to be big fans of partnerships between citizens and government, they showed little interest in anything beyond tightly controlled citizen involvement as a way of managing public perceptions and containing dissent.

If people in Vancouver wanted to see more meaningful citizen involvement, so did residents of many other cities. To make the handbook more widely available a number of volunteers with the Vancouver Community Net produced a web version of *The Citizen's Handbook*. This version, now at *www.vcn.bc.ca/citizens-handbook*, remains one of the few complete grassroots organizing guides available on the internet.

Like its precursor, *The Troublemaker's Teaparty* is meant for small citizens groups with little or no funding. Most of the literature on citizen action ignores small citizens groups and focuses on larger, funded nonprofits with staff.

The Troublemaker's Teaparty extends *The Citizen's Handbook* to include material that is missing from most manuals on grassroots organizing and community development. For instance, most ignore the hidden rocks and whirlpools that frequently wreck the plans of ordinary citizens new to public involvement. The beaming optimism of so many of these books sets citizens up for failure and inevitable retreat back into private life. This volume identifies the rocks and whirlpools and suggests practical ways to avoid them.

This book also addresses the broader dimensions of public action. While it continues to emphasize local improvement, it contains new material to help guide citizen action focused on issues affecting a larger commons, and those affecting people living in other places. Chapters 1 to 6 focus on place-based community action, while Chapters 7 to 10 shift the focus to public interest action that transcends place. The book contains these additions:

- A range of tactics spanning cooperation, negotiation, campaigning, and confrontation, and when to use them

- More material on small group dynamics, because small groups must be able to manage themselves effectively without the help of professionals

- Tips on the best ways to nudge government; while democratic governments may behave badly or incompetently, they are still the best allies of citizens interested in public interest issues

- A large collection of community-building projects citizens can use to build local community and enhance social place

- New ideas for getting noticed (Access to the mainstream media has always been a problem for grassroots groups. Now there are ways to bypass corporate control of the media.)

- A guide to strategic thinking

- Answers to the basic questions of organizing:
  How do we get others involved?
  How do we respect different views, but work cooperatively?
  How do we decide what is important?
  How do we define actions that will achieve what is important?
  How do we find necessary time and resources?
  How can we contribute modestly and still make a difference?

- A summary of research into what works for social movements

I have tried to avoid entering into a polemic on topical issues such as globalization, poverty, and environmental protection, which dilutes so many books on citizen action. I assume you understand your issue and are trying to figure out how to make progress.

I have also tried to eliminate unnecessary words, because activists would rather be acting than reading. Because *The Teaparty* is a manual, it lacks the repetition needed for skimming. The downside of this is that some readers will miss essentials by treating it like a long-winded work of non-fiction. *The Teaparty* should not be skimmed or read cover to cover, but rather consulted selectively according to what is happening at the moment.

Many thanks to Karen Hemmingson, Paula Carr, David Beers, Chris Warren, and Don Alexander for commenting on the manuscript.

Finally, I should say that this book is less the product of my expertise than of the expertise of many others. Think of it as a distillation of what we know about citizen action from the very best troublemakers.

Introduction

Why we need more active citizens

A T THE BEGINNING OF THE NEW MILLENNIUM we face a range of large and difficult problems. What we need to address these problems are more active citizens – people motivated by an interest in public issues, and a desire to make a difference beyond their own private lives. Active citizens are a great untapped resource, and citizenship is a quality to be nurtured. Here's why.

A Way of Tackling Large Public Issues. Those who have studied health, social, and environmental problems generally conclude that progress will only come with more active citizens. Many problems are too large, complex, and expensive to be addressed by government alone. Most require the consent of the majority of the electorate before government feels it can act. On difficult issues this often means people have to become involved to the point where they can make choices based on an understanding of the different consequences of different courses of action.

A Way of Solving Local Problems. When people become involved in their own neighborhoods they can become a potent force for dealing with local problems. With coordinated planning, research, and action, they can accomplish what individuals working alone could not. When they begin to work with other individuals, schools, associations, businesses, and government service providers, there is no limit to what they can accomplish.

A Way of Improving Livability. Citizens can make cities work better because they understand their own neighborhoods better than anyone else. Giving them some responsibility for looking after their part of town is a good way to address local preferences and priorities. Understandably, boosting citizen participation improves livability. It is no coincidence that Portland, Oregon – a city with a tradition of working in partnership with neighborhoods – regularly receives the highest score for livability of any US city.

A Way of Reducing Conflict. Cities are sources of potential conflict, between government and citizens, between one citizens group and another, and between citizens and business. Recent studies have shown that greater citizen participation in public affairs can reduce all of these sources of conflict. In particular, it can prevent the firestorms associated with changes brought about by growth and renewal.

A Bridge to Strong Democracy. When citizens get together at the neighborhood level, they generate a number of remarkable side effects. One of these is strengthened democracy. In simple terms, democracy means the people decide. Contrary to popular belief, building democracy in the West is an unfinished project. Political scientists describe our system of voting every few years but otherwise leaving everything up to government as weak democracy. In weak democracy, citizens have no role, no real part in decision making between elections. Experts decide how to deal with important public issues.

The great movement of the last decades of the twentieth century has been a drive toward stronger democracy in corporations, institutions, and governments. In many cities this has resulted in the formal recognition of neighborhood groups as a link between people and municipal government, and as a venue for citizen participation between elections.

A Little-Recognized Route to Better Health. In the late 1980s, following Canada's lead, the World Health Organization broadened its definition of health to account for the fact that health is much more than the absence of disease. The new definition recognizes that only 25 percent of our health status comes from health care; the rest comes from the effects of an adequate education and income, a clean environment, secure housing and employment, control over different aspects of our lives, and a social support network. Understandably, public health professionals have become some of the strongest advocates for more active citizens.

A Way of Rekindling Community. Active citizens can help to create a sense of community connected to place. We all live somewhere. As a result we share a unique collection of problems and prospects in common with our neighbors. Participation in neighborhood affairs builds on a recognition of here-we-are-together and a yearning to recapture something of the tight-knit communities of the past. Neighborhood groups can act as vehicles for making face-to-face connections between people, as forums for resolving local differences, and as a means of looking after one another. Most important, they can create a positive social environment that becomes one of the best features of a place.

When citizens become active in their own communities they often become involved in issues that transcend place. They become active in "communities of interest" that not only address regional, national, and international issues but also connect people who live in different places, promoting a breadth of empathy and understanding that is difficult to achieve in any other way.

A Way of Balancing a Bias for Privacy. Market economies are heavily biased in favor of privacy. When people lead private lives they spend more time consuming market products and less time consuming social products. A marketplace economy prefers to have everyone living alone. When a couple splits up it means they will need twice as many beds, stoves, washing machines, microwaves, computers, TVs, cars, couches, and so forth. A culture that promotes privacy is good for business, but it's not good for people. Studies on happiness show that the most important factor in determining happiness is the number and depth of human relationships.

A Way of Increasing Social Capital. One important aspect of a civil society is the degree to which people rise above narrow self-interest (selfish behavior) and function for the greater good of the community. For civil society to exist, its participants must develop trust in one another – enough trust to allow society to function without elaborate sets of rules and laws.

We do favors for one another with the expectation that in due course the "debt" will be repaid. These are not selfish expectations but rather the behaviors that maintain civil institutions like churches, teams, clubs, and organizations that depend on donors and volunteers. These behaviors rely upon the norms of reciprocity. According to Robert Putnam, author of *Bowling Alone: The Collapse and Revival of American Community*, "social capital refers to connections among individuals – social networks and the norms of reciprocity and trustworthiness that arise from them."

But there are two types of reciprocity. The first is specific reciprocity: "I'll scratch your back; you scratch mine." Participants engage in an exchange which both perceive as equal at the time the transaction takes place. Specific reciprocity produces connections between people that exist largely for the moment.

The second and more valuable type is generalized reciprocity, which creates connections that last over time. According to Putnam, it is more a case of: "I'll scratch your back because sooner or later you, or someone within our social network, will likely scratch mine. A society characterized by generalized reciprocity is more efficient than a distrustful society, for the same reason that money is more efficient than barter. If we don't have to balance every exchange instantly, we can get a lot more accomplished. Trustworthiness lubricates social life."

But what are the tangible benefits of higher social capital? Putnam's conservative assessment of research on the subject shows they are profound. Kids are better off; schools work better; government works better;

violent crime is less; people are less pugnacious; economic equality is higher; civic equality is higher; and tolerance is higher.

Social capital derives roughly from the amount of political engagement, the density of social networks, the level of participation in religious and civic organizations, and the degree of social trust. Putnam shows that most of the measurable indicators of social trust in the US are *declining*. This includes:

- declining membership in civic groups like the Lions and the Kiwanis,
- declining participation in political campaign activities,
- declining attendance at public meetings,
- declining church attendance,
- declining membership in unions and professional organizations,
- less social visiting,
- less entertaining at home,
- less time during the workday devoted to informal socializing,
- less charitable giving,
- fewer family dinners,
- declining attendance at rallies,
- fewer letters to the editor, and
- declining membership in clubs and leagues (the title of Putnam's book refers to the precipitous decline of bowling leagues, even though participation in bowling itself remains high).

Nevertheless Putnam is optimistic we can reverse the steady decline in social capital if we can find effective ways to nurture civic engagement and increase the number of active citizens. In the following chapters I hope to spell out the practical details of moving in this direction.

CHAPTER 1

Community Organizing

THIS CHAPTER PROVIDES a do-it-yourself guide to grassroots organizing. It focuses on bringing together people who share a common place such as an apartment building, city block, or neighborhood. Most of the material also applies to organizing around an issue.

Organizing is the effort of pulling together a group of unconnected people to work toward some common goal.

1.1   Before You Begin

Before you begin organizing, you should gauge the size of your task, and the amount of your resources. The big problem for grassroots organizing is resources, particularly time. Organizing a block or two to address a local problem is manageable for one or two people. Larger areas and difficult problems can take over the life of a do-it-yourself organizer.

A paid organizer, when you can't do it all yourself

A paid, experienced organizer can help when the task is to pull citizens together quickly or in large numbers. A paid organizer may be the only option when there is no one able or willing to take on the task as a volunteer. Paid organizers seem to be needed for low-income neighborhoods and for groups like seniors.

Paid organizers often begin by gathering information on the neighborhood, then proceed by introducing themselves to residents, bringing people together in discussion groups, building self-help skills, and, finally, training new leaders to take over the organizing task. Many organizers will door-knock in order to ask a carefully constructed set of questions aimed at motivating people to get involved. Questions may help people see that something is very wrong. Or they may help people realize they have been mistreated. In the end the organizer has to give people the confidence that they can solve whatever problem they face.

The presence of a professional organizer may lead some volunteers to wonder why they are working for free while someone else is being paid. A few groups have addressed this problem by converting funds for an organizer into honoraria for volunteers.

Finding an organizer might be difficult. In the United States there are many training programs in community organizing. The Industrial Areas Foundation (IAF), the Midwest Academy, Antioch, the Association of Community Organizations for Reform Now (ACORN), and the Highlander Center are some of the better known. In Canada, there are almost none. Canadians' faith in government has placed decisions about their communities in the hands of politicians and professionals.

Adapt to available resources

Most of the organizing methods described in this chapter will be easy if you have resources, particularly money for a paid organizer. Some will be very difficult if you have no resources. Most of the literature on community development is far too optimistic about what can be achieved by all-volunteer groups that are not propelled by a hot issue. With no resources you need to:

- reduce the amount of time devoted to what seems like work,
- keep the group size small,
- weave actions into everyday life,
- make sure everyone enjoys one another's company, and
- focus on a single short project with concrete results, or on a single long project with good potential for concrete results along the way.

When trying a new dish, the best cooks don't follow any recipe precisely. Instead, they look at a number of related recipes, then adapt to available resources – ingredients on hand and the amount of time. You should treat any recipe for community organizing the same way: as a guide for action that you will modify to fit available resources and actual circumstances.

1.2   Beginning

Where do you begin if you want to become more involved in public life or the public life of your neighborhood? Here are some options.

Begin with research. Although professionals often start with research about an issue, you don't have to start here. On the other hand, you might be wise to begin with research if you intend to tackle an issue you do not fully understand. If your focus is local, talking to local politicians and people in local organizations is a good way to begin research.

Begin with a community building activity. Chapters 4 and 5 contain a large collection of projects for bringing people together.

Begin by joining an existing group. Most neighborhoods or communities have many different kinds of active organizations. Linking up with one of these can be an easy way to get involved. Begin by checking out the groups listed on your city's website under the heading Community Organizations or Neighborhood Organizations.

Begin by starting a new group. If working with an existing group looks difficult, you might have to start a new group. New organizations usually form around a core of three to five committed people. Putting together a core of first-rate people is worth the effort.

A core group should consider these questions:

- What are we trying to do?
- What size of area are we going to organize?
- Who will support our efforts?
- What is a good idea for our first action? (It should be simple, focus on a local concern, and increase the group's visibility.)
- How are we going to reach out to others?
- Should we organize a big meeting and invite the community?

Make a special effort to remain friendly with other local groups that have similar goals. Friendliness can help cooperation prevail over the tendency to compete. Intergroup cooperation is the engine of real progress at the grassroots.

1.3   Forming a Core Group

Forming a core group is the single most important part of creating a new community group or public interest group. A core group without funds or staff should stay small. It should not expand beyond ten people – what sociologists call a primary group. For groups that do intend to grow, the core initially sets the direction of the group, makes most decisions, and does most of the work. Because members of a core group usually spend a lot of time together, they should be people who enjoy one another's company.

Never open the door to all comers

The makeup of the core will determine the friendliness, effectiveness, and longevity of the group, so don't open the door to just anyone, and don't extend an open invitation to anyone who wants to join. Instead, carefully choose friendly, keen people with a record of getting things done. If you must open the door to general membership, do so after you have an effective core group in place.

No doubt this advice will set off alarm bells for anyone trained in community development, where unreserved openness and inclusivity have become a mantra. In an ideal world, every group would be completely open and inclusive. In practice, small groups with no external support tend to break up when they include people who are incompetent, unreliable, or simply unpleasant. See 6.10 "Grassroots Wilt 4."

Decide what kind of group you want to be

Different grassroots groups have different reasons for getting together. This book is mainly intended for public interest groups, meaning groups that are interested in providing public goods to more than their own members. For public interest groups the first consideration is defining the public good. Is it preserving native fish, preventing teen drug addiction, or something else?

Grassroots groups also have different styles, partly because of the nature of their members and partly because of the nature of their work. Public interest groups range from those that try to provide a public good themselves, to those that try to get government or someone else to provide the public good. The first kind of group might clear streams for fish habitat or arrange for former teen drug addicts to talk in high schools. The second kind of group might campaign for stronger laws protecting streams or agitate for a program to prevent teen drug addiction. The first six chapters of this book are intended mainly for the first kind of group; the final chapters are for the second kind of group.

Decide what kind of people you want

If you are fighting a battle against a large company, you might want a corporate lawyer from your community, a communications expert for signs and flyers, and a labor organizer to mobilize the community. A different kind of group might want people who are well-connected to the community, to political leaders, or to business leaders. A group that gets together for conversation will want people who are friendly, well-read, and knowledgeable. A group that takes on social change projects will be interested in creative people with activist backgrounds and strategic thinking abilities.

Look for people who are:

- Smart
- Keen and energetic
- Available
- Sparky (good at taking the initiative)
- Inclined to humor
- Reliable and determined
- Friendly and cooperative
- Natural leaders
- Skilled where skills are needed

Find the right people

There are several ways to find the right people for your core group. Most involve identifying prospects, then arranging lunch or a follow-up meeting to get to know them better. You may already know people who fit your criteria. If you don't know anyone, you may know someone who does. You can hold a community meeting and survey participants. This is a good way to proceed if the community is faced with a problem. Natural leaders tend to come forward. If skills are important, ask prospects what they do for a living. Get the names and phone numbers of the best prospects; then arrange to meet.

Once you identify good people, ask them to join the core group.

With a good core group, everything else falls into place. If the objective is to address a community problem, the core group will have to figure out how to keep everyone else informed about what's going on, and at least slightly involved.

1.4   Getting to Know One Another

The most elementary achievement of community development is the connection between two people where none had previously existed. If we go back to this basic building block we can see what is wrong with a lot of traditional community development. It does not make good connections between people because it does not set aside time for people to get to know one another. Sure, people might know each other's names and why they are involved, but they rarely get much further. Because most community groups get together to address a problem, the focus quickly shifts from understanding one another to dealing with the problem at hand.

Make time at your first meeting for a getting-to-know-one-another exercise. Remind action-oriented participants who object to the time needed for this exercise that good relationships between people will make action easier and sustainable.

A getting-to-know-one-another exercise

This exercise suits a group of about ten. It begins with people choosing partners. Each person in turn takes five minutes to tell their partner about themselves. You might talk about:

- Your heroes
- Your career history
- The worst, or funniest, or thing you did last year
- What makes you different from other people
- What most influenced you or affected your life
- Your passions
- Relationships with others, including problems

Try to reveal essentials about yourself. Listeners should ask follow-up questions. Some people may be reluctant to reveal "private" information, but this is what is required. Once partners have heard one another's stories, the group reconvenes, and the listeners take one minute to summarize their partner's story for the rest of the group.

1.5 Getting More People

If your group has no staff and no funding, limit the size to about 10 people. Large groups are too difficult to manage without resources and soon fall apart. Small volunteer groups should stay small and focus on getting a broader public involved only occasionally in events, workshops, or community building projects that help to achieve a specific objective. For these occasions, small groups can attract people by offering something that does not seem like work – activities that are exciting, entertaining, educational, or socially stimulating.

The approach is different for funded groups. Getting more people is usually an important ongoing activity because volunteers are needed for regular day-to-day operations and often undertake the routine work of fundraising, mailing, answering the phone, and so forth. Because it is not easy to get people to do this kind of work in their spare time, funded organizations devote a lot of resources to recruiting and keeping volunteers.

Ask members to invite others. People won't get involved unless asked, so if you want to get more people, encourage more person-to-person asking. Eighty percent of volunteers doing community work said they began because they were asked by a friend, a family member, or a neighbor.

Go to where people are. Instead of trying to get people to come to you, try going to them. Go to the meetings of other groups; go to the places and events where people gather. This is particularly important for ethnic groups, youth groups, seniors, and other groups that are unlikely to come to you.

Tap existing networks. The Industrial Areas Foundation has been very successful at getting lots of people involved by weaving itself into existing church networks – see Appendix 1. Regular Sunday gatherings of thousands of people present endless opportunities for getting things done. Cohesive networks provide the best opportunities, but looser networks focused on schools and colleges, professional associations, umbrella cultural and ethnic associations, recreational and business groups, and unions offer ways to systematically involve large numbers of people.

Collect names, addresses, e-mail addresses, phone numbers. Have sign-in sheets at your meetings and events. At public hearings and open houses, collect information by having sign-up sheets near the front door for people who want to receive the results of your group's independent research.

Use petitions to gather names and numbers. An easy way to gather names and contact information is to ask people to sign a petition. Have the petition available at rallies, protests, public meetings, conferences, and so forth. The list can be used to recruit people for other actions. In fact, a good list is often the most valuable product because petitions themselves often achieve little.

Address the weakest person-situation variable. Psychologist Walter Mischel argues that five "person-situation" variables determine how we will act in any given situation. These variables also determine the likelihood of involvement in a citizens group:
- Skills – what can I do?
- View of the situation – How bad is the problem?
- Expectations – How much can I actually expect to accomplish?
- Values – How important is this situation to me?
- Personal standards – Is it my duty ?

Figuring out which of these variables most contributes to lack of involvement can help an organizer figure out how to get more people. For instance, if people don't think they have the necessary skills, an organizer might run workshops to develop them.

Try to include those who are under-represented. Minority language groups, low-income residents, the disabled, the elderly, and youth all tend to be under-represented in neighborhood activities. In some cases, not participating is a matter of choice – most transient youth choose not to take part. In other cases, English language competence poses a formidable barrier to participation. In still other cases, people get overlooked; the elderly are often ignored, even though they can contribute a great deal because they have extra time.

Ways to include the under-represented:

- Go to people in the group you are trying to reach and ask how they would like to be approached. Then address their issues.

- Think about who you know who knows someone in the group you are trying to reach. Use your connections.

- Identify a group as people you want to work with, not as a target group you want to bring "on side." Treat people as people first.

Organize projects that focus on kids. If children are involved in an activity, parents will often get involved. This helps to build community, as people of different ethnic backgrounds and income levels will meet one another while accompanying their children.

Do surveys. Surveys are a good way to stay in touch, increase participation, and bring in new members. They show your group is working with a broad base of people, not just those who tend to participate in community activities.

Door-knock. Door-knocking is one of the oldest and best outreach methods. See 1.6 "Door-knocking" for more information.

Generate newsletters and leaflets. Newsletters keep group members in touch. Because most neighborhood groups deliver to all residents, whether they are members or not, a newsletter helps attract new people. For tips see 1.12 "Information Sharing."

Create detailed membership lists

Create membership lists with places for entering name, address, e-mail, day and evening phone and fax numbers, priorities for local improvement, occupation, personal interests, special skills, times available, what the person would be willing to do, and what the person would *not* be willing to do. Consider using a computer to update lists and sort people by address, priority, and interests. With such a computer database you can easily bring together people with common interests.

Membership lists can also form the basis of a telephone tree, a system for getting messages out to large numbers of people. For tips on setting up a telephone tree see 1.12 "Information Sharing."

1.6   Door-Knocking

Door-knocking is the most effective way of making face-to-face community contact, but it has become a lost art. With commercial culture's bias for privacy, door-knocking seems like an intrusion into other people's lives. But those who try it for the first time are usually surprised by the pleasant reception they receive. Here are some door-knocking pointers.

Before you go out

If you can afford it, leave a door-hanger two days before you go door-knocking. It will prepare people for a visit, and it can introduce an unusual project. The door-hanger should briefly describe the project and say that someone will be around in person. Make the door-hanger with light cardstock, cut about 5.5 by 8.5 inches, with a 1.5-inch hole cut in the top and a slit on the side of the hole. A less expensive but less effective alternative is a notice put through the letter-slot.

Wear an official name tag. Door-knockers should wear name tags with the logo of their organization. The logo should match the logo on any door-hanger. The best name tags will also include a color photo and the name of the canvasser. Name tags are especially important in neighborhoods where people might be suspicious of someone knocking on the door.

Have people knock their own blocks. The easiest way to do door-knocking is to do your own block. This allows door-knockers to use an introduction like: "My name is Jill Smith and I live in the green house three doors down from you." Being a neighbor creates an immediate bond with the person answering the door; after that everything else is easy. Arranging for people to knock their own block is the basis of a lot of grassroots organizing.

A survey is a good excuse to door-knock. If you simply want to connect to people, consider preparing a short survey about local concerns, a current project, or your group's goals.

Figure out responses for various situations. What if no one is home? What if the person who answers the door cannot speak English? What if a child answers the door? Figuring out responses ahead of time will make door-knocking easier.

When you go out

The best times to knock are any time on Saturdays, and other days between dinner and darkness. When someone answers the door, smile and introduce yourself; say you are a volunteer and if it helps say where you live. Give the name of your organization and, briefly, the reason for the visit. Ask if the person might have a minute to talk. If the answer is yes, state the reason for your visit in more detail.

Bring out links between yourself and the other person. Mention where you live if you live on the same block. Otherwise, bring up something that links the two of you to your project. For instance, a person knocking to obtain support for better child protection might begin: "Do you remember when they found that small boy who had been left alone for four days. . ?"

State what action the other person should take. Ideally this is an action this person can take on the spot.

State the benefits of taking the action. Tell the person how their actions will benefit themselves and others.

If a person hesitates. . . Emphasize benefits you've already mentioned and then, if necessary, add further benefits. If the person continues to hesitate, offer a more limited form of action. Lee Staples recommends this approach for door-to-door fundraising in his book on grassroots organizing, *Roots to Power.* He says start off asking for a lot, then step back to something more modest.

If a person agrees, follow up immediately. If possible, get a donation, a signature, a pledge. For actions that take place at a later date, you should follow up with a phone call reminder. You could also ask about time commitments and resources or expertise a person might be able to contribute to a project.

Record contact information on the spot. Record names, addresses, e-mail addresses, phone numbers, and responses to questions on the spot. For additional suggestions on door-knocking, see the comprehensive Community Toolbox created by the University of Kansas, available on-line at *http://ctb.lsi.ukans.edu/.*

1.7   Block-by-Block Organizing

The goal of organizing a neighborhood is to get everyone working together to address common concerns. You can organize a whole neighborhood without any external resources if residents are of high socio-economic status.

If residents are less well-off, you will probably need outside funding, extra time, and possibly a paid organizer. You may be able to get funding from a local community foundation or from a local government that recognizes the value of hearing from everyone, not just those who are well-off. In the US, you can obtain helpful advice from numerous national organizations such as the Association of Community Organizations for Reform Now (ACORN) and the Industrial Areas Foundation (IAF). See also 1.13 "Fundraising."

Block-by-block organizing usually begins with door-knocking. A small core group door-knocks to find block reps for every block in the area. A block can either be a block of houses, an apartment block, a co-op, or a condominium complex. Block reps introduce residents to one another, usually by inviting everyone to a backyard or common-room gathering. When neighbors first meet, they are often surprised and delighted to discover how many interesting people live on their own block.

In addition to bringing people together, block reps can also promote mutual aid. At the block level, mutual aid can range from dealing with a noisy neighbor to finding someone who will look after your cat while you are on vacation. The side effect of these small exchanges is a sense of community.

Once residents know one another, they can decide to accept the block rep who brought them together or elect a new block rep. Block reps then elect neighborhood reps, who get together to form a coordinating committee for a larger area. This simple organization can easily connect many people over an entire city. Neighbors meet with a focus on their block; block reps with a focus on the neighborhood; neighborhood reps with a focus on their local area. At the top level, a group of local area reps can focus on the city and meet to discuss such matters as budget priorities.

While the groups that meet regularly at every level are small, those above the block level require support because their tasks are more complex and more numerous. Local governments that see the benefits of working in partnership with citizens will often provide the modest support required.

Tips for organizing block by block

- Make the task manageable by focusing on small neighborhoods – no more than 10 blocks each.

- Encourage each block to act independently. Only when a problem is too large or difficult for a single block should people from other blocks become involved.

- Organize in twos, so each block has two block reps and each neighborhood has two neighborhood reps. This provides friendly support, improves information exchange, and reduces workloads.

- Consider integrating with Block Watch. Block Watch treats a block as opposite sides of the lane, while block-by-block organizing treats a block as opposite sides of the street. Despite the difference, the two patterns of organizing can support one another.

1.8   Organizing Around an Issue

People often organize around a single issue. They get together because they are annoyed or angry about street prostitution, extra taxes, the loss of a wilderness area, or an ugly development scheme. Often the issue is a proposed change or addition to the neighborhood that is seen as undesirable. Developers, whose business is change, often describe this kind of activism as NIMBYism (Not-In-My-Back-Yard syndrome), a selfish attempt by residents to keep their part of town just as it is, in defiance of some larger public good such as a more compact city. Developers ignore the fact that the first towns arose out of the natural tendency for people to band together to oppose disruptive outsiders.

For activists, the threat of unwanted development can have a silver lining. It can be just what is needed to bring people together.

But organizing around a hot issue can waste huge amounts of time and drive people apart if it begins with hardened positions. Too often citizens wear themselves out in fights that might have been resolved to everyone's satisfaction through collaborative problem solving that focuses on interests rather than positions. See 2.4 "Mediation and Conflict Resolution."

Until recently, most of the books written about community organizing have taken a battlefield approach because it was the only way to influence public decision making. In many cases it is still the quickest way to get results. But it has one big problem. After an issue is resolved, everyone retreats back into private life.

1.9   Keeping People Involved

People join community groups to meet people, to have fun, to learn new skills, to pursue an interest, and to link their lives to some higher purpose. They leave if they don't find what they are looking for.

Citizens groups need to ask themselves the following questions more often:

- What benefits do we provide?
- At what cost to members?
- How can we increase the benefits and decrease the costs?

Here are some ways to increase benefits and keep people involved.

Stay in touch with one another. Regular contact is vital. Getting together once a week is common for small action-oriented groups in the midst of a project. Groups that do not provide a regular way for people to stay in touch usually fall apart.

Welcome newcomers. Larger, funded groups often have a paid coordinator of volunteers who makes newcomers feel welcome, makes it easy for them to contribute, and ensures their work is appreciated. A coordinator of volunteers should call new contacts, invite them to events, and try to promote relationships between the newcomers and "insiders." Newcomers should be able to assume leadership roles. If the same people run everything, newcomers feel excluded.

A coordinator of volunteers should also help people find a place in the organization. The most appealing approach is to say: "Tell us the things you like to do and do well and we will find a way to use those talents." The next most appealing is to say: "Here are the jobs we have, but *how* you get them done is up to you."

Pay attention to group process. Most volunteer groups do not give adequate attention to how they work together. Decision-making methods are not determined explicitly, nor are roles or healthy behaviors. Some larger, funded groups make process a topic of discussion by appointing a process watcher. See 1.11 "Facilitating" and Chapter 2.

Discuss the group contract. Set aside occasions when members describe what they expect of the group and what the group can expect of them in terms of time and responsibilities.

Act more, meet less. The great majority of people detest meetings; too many are the Black Death of community groups. By comparison, community activities like tree-planting draw large numbers of people of all ages.

Keep time demands modest. Most people lead busy lives. Don't ask them to come to housekeeping meetings if they don't need to be there. Work out realistic time commitments for projects, and flexible work schemes that people can adapt to their own schedules. Try to figure out ways of combining elements of everyday life (dining, exercising, working, traveling, learning, child-minding, gardening, and other forms of recreation) with public interest activities. Don't force people to choose between civic engagement and family life. A good project combines both.

> **A street tree project**
>
> Tree-planting projects are very popular because they combine civic engagement with normal family activities: gardening, learning, and child-minding. Families first learn how to plant and care for a tree. The next day they dig the holes and plant the trees delivered by the city. After that, family members look after the trees by providing water whenever it is needed.

Spread out the work. Larger, funded organizations should keep expanding the number of active members to ensure everyone does a little and no one does too much.

Do it in twos. Working in pairs improves the quality of communication, makes work less lonely, and ensures tasks get done. Ethnically mixed pairs (such as English and Chinese) can establish links between different cultures. Gender mixed pairs can take advantage of differences in ways of relating to men and women.

Provide skills training. Larger, funded groups should provide skill-building workshops and on-the-job training. Simply pairing experienced and inexperienced people will improve the skills of new members. Training in leadership, group facilitating, and conflict resolution is important enough to warrant special weekend workshops. For more on keeping people, see Chapters 2 and 6.

1.10   Leading

Good leaders are the key to large-scale community organizing. They do not tell other people what to do, but help others to take charge. They do not grab center stage, but nudge others into the limelight. They are not interested in being The Leader, but in trying to create more leaders. They recognize that only by creating more leaders can an organizing effort expand. For more on leaders see Appendix 1.

Lead by creating an example to follow. Some leaders are larger-than-life heroes. Some deliver inspirational speeches. Others are excellent organizers. But many leaders inspire others to follow by setting an example. When Rosa Parks refused to give up a bus seat reserved for white people, others followed her example in such numbers that it blossomed into the civil rights movement.

Divide-up and delegate work. Divide tasks into bite-sized chunks, then discuss who will do each chunk. Make sure everyone has the ability to carry out their task, then let them carry it out in their own way. Have someone check on progress. People do not feel good about doing a job if nobody cares whether it gets done.

Appreciate all contributions, no matter how small. Recognize people's efforts in conversations, at meetings, in newsletters, and with tokens of appreciation: thank-you notes, certificates, and awards for special efforts.

Welcome criticism. Accepting criticism may be difficult for some leaders, but members need to feel they can be critical without being attacked.

Help people to believe in themselves. A leader builds people's confidence that they can accomplish what they have never accomplished before. The unflagging optimism of a good leader energizes everyone.

Light-up people. Good leaders energize people through their own energy and enthusiasm. To combat apathy and disengagement they often combine an energetic attack on the status quo with an enthusiastic description of how to make things better.

Inspire trust. People will not follow those they do not trust. Always maintain the highest standards of honesty. Good leaders reveal their potential conflicts of interest and air doubts about their own personal limitations.

Herald a higher purpose. People often volunteer to serve some higher purpose. A leader should be able to articulate this purpose, to hold it up as a glowing beacon whenever the occasion demands. A good leader will celebrate every grassroots victory as an example of what can happen when people work together for a common good.

Heralding a higher purpose may require some practice at heralding. Recognized leaders are usually good at public speaking. In Canada, a surprising number of activist leaders belong to Toastmasters!

Avoid doing most of the work. Don't try to run the whole show or do most of the work. Others will become less involved. And you will burn out.

1.11 Meeting

Meetings are necessary for collective thinking, planning, and decision making. Unfortunately, many meetings are run badly.

The basics of meeting

Fix a convenient time, date, and place to meet. You can find free meeting places in libraries, community centers, some churches, neighborhood houses, and schools. Some groups meet in a favorite restaurant or café. To keep a group together, fix a regular meeting time or think of another way to stay in touch, such as an e-mail newsletter.

Agree on an agenda beforehand. A good agenda states meeting place; starting time, time allocated for each item, ending time; objectives of the meeting; and items to be discussed. Meetings that address uncontroversial matters should move at a brisk pace.

Start the meeting by choosing a facilitator, a recorder, and a timekeeper. Begin with a round of introductions if necessary. Next, review the record of what was decided at the previous meeting. Ask for amendments or additions to the agenda, then begin working through the agenda. If you have trouble reaching agreement, refer to 1.11 "Decision Making."

The recorder should note what actions are required to carry out plans and decisions, who will carry them out, and how much will be accomplished before the next meeting. Finally, set a time, place, and agenda for the next meeting.

Follow a set of discussion guidelines. Regular meetings work better if everyone agrees on a set of discussion guidelines. Some groups post their guidelines as a large sign:

Listen to others

Do not interrupt

Ask clarifying questions

Welcome new ideas

Forego personal attacks

Develop a friendly culture. Treat every contribution as valuable. Consider having the recorder display everyone's contributions using a flip chart, projector, or blackboard. Provide food and drink. Allow for social time. Encourage humor. Meetings should be lively and as much fun as possible.

Decision making

Your group should discuss, agree on, and occasionally review guidelines for reaching decisions. Some of the basic methods of decision making are described below.

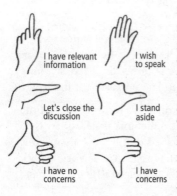

I have relevant information

I wish to speak

Let's close the discussion

I stand aside

I have no concerns

I have concerns

Straw polling. Straw polling involves asking for a show of hands to see how the group feels about a particular issue. It is a quick check that can save a great deal of time. To make straw polling continuous, some groups agree on a set of hand signals everyone will use throughout the meeting. These silent signals enable people to gauge how others are reacting moment by moment. They can also provide invaluable feedback for a speaker who is trying to work with a large group.

Voting. Voting is a decision-making method that seems best suited to large groups. To avoid alienating large minorities, you might decide a motion will only succeed with a two-thirds majority. Alternatively, you might decide to combine voting with consensus (see below). Small groups usually follow informal consensus procedures. Large groups, on the other hand, often try to follow *Robert's Rules of Order*, often without anyone really understanding how to *amend a motion* or knowing the number of people needed to *move the question*. If rules are used, they should be simple and understood by everyone.

Some community groups limit the privilege of voting to people who have come to three or more consecutive meetings. This prevents stacked meetings and encourages familiarity with the issues being decided.

Voting usually means deciding between X or Y – but not always. Some issues will admit a proportional solution, part X and part Y. In such cases the ratio of X to Y in the solution usually reflects the ratio of people voting for each alternative.

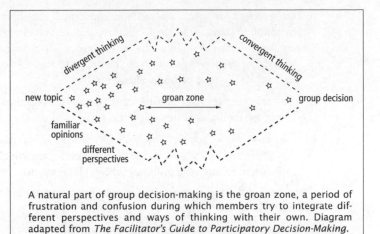

divergent thinking

convergent thinking

new topic ☆   groan zone   ☆ group decision

familiar
opinions

different
perspectives

A natural part of group decision-making is the groan zone, a period of frustration and confusion during which members try to integrate different perspectives and ways of thinking with their own. Diagram adapted from *The Facilitator's Guide to Participatory Decision-Making*.

Consensus. A consensus process aims at bringing the group to mutual agreement by addressing all concerns. It does *not* require unanimity. In small groups, informal consensus is the most common form of decision making. In large groups consensus can take longer than other processes, but it fosters creativity, cooperation, and commitment to final decisions. Consensus always works better when combined with dialogue. See section 2.1 "Dialogue". Here is a sample outline of the process:

1. A presenter states the proposal. Ideally, a written draft has been distributed prior to the meeting.

2. The group discusses and clarifies the proposal. No one presents concerns until clarification is complete.

3. The facilitator asks for legitimate concerns. If there are none the facilitator asks the group if it has reached consensus.

4. If there are concerns, the recorder lists the concerns where everyone can see them.

5. The group tries to resolve concerns. The presenter has first option to:
   - Clarify the proposal
   - Change the proposal
   - Explain why it is not in conflict with the group's values
   - Ask those with concerns to stand aside. By "standing aside" a person indicates a willingness to live with a proposal. By "crossing off a concern" a person indicates satisfaction with clarifications or changes.

COMMUNITY ORGANIZING 23

6. If concerns remain unresolved and concerned members are unwilling to stand aside, the facilitator asks everyone to examine these concerns in relation to the group's purpose and values. The group may need to go through a special session to examine its purpose or resolve value conflicts.

7. The facilitator checks again to see if those with concerns are willing to stand aside or cross off their concerns.

8. If they are not willing to stand aside or cross off concerns, the facilitator keeps asking for suggestions to resolve the concerns until everyone finds the proposal acceptable or stands aside.

Often the solution is a "third way," something between either/or, black or white.

If time runs out and concerns persist, the facilitator may:
- conduct a straw poll,
- ask those with concerns if they will stand aside,
- ask the presenter to withdraw the proposal,
- contract with the group for more time,
- send the proposal to a subgroup, or
- conduct a vote, needing a 75 per cent majority to pass.

9. At the end, the facilitator states the outcome clearly.

For consensus to work properly, everyone must understand the meaning of "legitimate concerns." These are possible consequences of the proposal that might adversely affect the organization or the common good, or that are in conflict with the purpose or values of the group.

Consensus will not work properly if concerns come from ego or vested interests, or derive from unstated tensions around authority, rights, personality conflicts, competition, or lack of trust. Trust is a prerequisite for consensus.

If your group adopts consensus as a decision-making method, you do not have to use consensus of the whole group to decide everything. You can (and should) empower individuals, committees, or task forces to make certain decisions.

Live with disagreements. Get agreement on the big picture, then turn to action. Don't exhaust yourself trying to achieve consensus on details. If you acknowledge a variety of positions on a contentious issue, you will suffer fewer attacks and encourage flexibility from those who tend toward hardened positions.

Facilitating

The facilitator's role is to help a group do its best thinking. A good facilitator is helpful when a group is trying to deal with new or difficult issues. In the main, a facilitator helps people persevere as they confront the inevitable confusion and frustration associated with trying to integrate different views and approaches with their own. The more people who learn to facilitate, the better. If you accept the role of facilitator you must be neutral. You should also try to follow good facilitating practices:

Watch group vibes. If people seem bored or inattentive, you may have to speed up the pace of the meeting. If people seem tense because of unvoiced disagreements, you may have to bring concerns out into the open.

Make sure everyone gets a chance to speak. Invite quiet people to speak. If necessary, use the clock: "We have fifteen minutes left. I think we should hear from people who haven't spoken for a while." Another way to get quiet people to speak is to initiate a round, in which you move around the table, with everyone getting a few minutes to present their views.

Encourage open discussion. Try to encourage people to speak up if they seem reluctant to disagree with a speaker: "On difficult issues, people disagree. Does anyone have a different point of view?" Another way to encourage open discussion is to ask participants to avoid using critical language for a period of time.

Draw people out with open-ended questions. Open-ended questions require more than a yes/no answer.

- *We seem to be having trouble. What do you think we should do?*
- *Could you say more about that?*
- *Why do you think that . . ?*
- *What do you mean when you say. . ?*

Inject humor. Humor is one of the best ways of improving the tone of meetings. It makes meetings seem like friendly get-togethers.

Paraphrase. Here you try to restate briefly the point that someone has just made: "Let me see if I'm understanding you. . ." If paraphrasing doesn't convince a person that he or she has been heard, you may have to repeat what was said verbatim.

Learn to deal with difficult behavior

Flare-ups: When two members get into a heated discussion, summarize the points made by each and then turn the discussion back to the group.

Grandstanding: Interrupt the one-person show with a statement that gives credit for his or her contribution, but ask the person to reserve other points for later.

Broken recording: Paraphrase the contribution of someone who repeats the same point over and over. This lets the person know the point has been heard.

Interrupting: Step in immediately. "Hold on, let Margaret finish what she has to say."

Continual criticizing: Legitimize negative feelings on difficult issues. You might say, "Yes, it will be tough to reduce traffic on Main Street, but there are successful models we can look at."

Identify areas of common ground. Summarize differences in points of view, then note where there is common ground. For instance, you might begin, "It seems we agree that. . ."

Follow a procedure to reach closure. One procedure for large groups is to ask the group to vote. A better procedure for small groups is for the person in charge to:

1. close the discussion,
2. clarify the proposal,
3. poll the group, then
4. decide to a) make the decision or b) continue the discussion.

Suggest options when time runs out. Identify areas of partial consensus, suggest tabling the question, or create a small subcommittee to deal with the matter at its convenience.

Consider a round at the end of the meeting. Going quickly around the whole group at the end of the meeting gives people a chance to bring up matters not on the agenda. You can also use a round to evaluate the meeting. With more than ten people, though, a round can become tedious.

Learn more about facilitating. Good facilitating is something to behold, but it is not magic. To learn more get a good guide, such as Sam Kaner's *Facilitator's Guide to Participatory Decision Making*.

1.12   Information Sharing

Once you have your group up and running, you need to devise ways to get information out to members or to the neighborhood. Perhaps you need to let people know about an event or action. Maybe you need to let people know what they missed at a meeting. Or perhaps you just want to keep people informed of what you're up to. Here are some ways to share information.

Knock and drop

How do you tell everyone in your neighborhood about an event they should attend? Many neighborhood associations do a "knock and drop." Block reps knock on doors to invite neighbors to attend; if no one is home, they drop off a leaflet. Other groups put up posters. Some photocopy machines can turn a leaflet into a small poster suitable for advertising in laundromats, community centers, and libraries. If you want people to attend your event, the best approach is to ask everyone to invite friends, family, and neighbors.

Newsletters

A newsletter is one of the most common ways for organizations that have resources to stay in touch. Community newsletters range in frequency from twice yearly to monthly. Most are printed on both sides of an 8.5 x 11 sheet or on both sides of a folded 11 x 17 sheet. Printing is either by high-speed photocopying or "instant" offset printing. You may be able to defray printing costs by enlisting the support of local merchants, local government, or community organizations.

The big job in putting out a newsletter is finding people who are willing and able to write articles that others are interested in reading. To get good newsletter content, a group often needs to find and pay a writer who will seek out good stories and write them up. Simply asking group members for submissions often yields few or poor results.

Besides a writer/researcher, you will need the skills of an editor and the services of a graphic designer to make your newsletter appear worth reading. Engaging newsletters look like newspapers, with narrow columns, photographs, and bold headlines.

You will also need people willing to arrange printing and distribution. Try to deliver your newsletter by hand – if you have block reps, they can easily deliver to their own block. Co-distribution is next best. This involves partnering with local schools, businesses, or community centers so that they distribute your newsletter with their own. Other distribution possibilities include schools sending the newsletter home with students; distribution in churches; literature distribution boxes in libraries, community centers, and other public places; ad mail; or a flyer distribution service. An e-mailed newsletter avoids the issue of distribution, but limits the audience to those who use e-mail.

Local newspapers

Local newspapers can also help with information sharing, although you may find that a local problem gets far more attention than a local solution. Fortunately, some small papers are changing their idea of what should go into a newspaper. They are beginning to publish articles with a positive local focus that are well written and worth reading.

Telephone trees

A telephone tree is a fast, person-to-person information-sharing technique. It requires a coordinator and a list of who calls whom. An outgoing message starts with the coordinator, who calls a pre-determined list of ten activators. The ten activators in turn each call another predetermined list of ten people, who in turn each call another ten. It is important to make sure those at the base of the tree are reliable. The coordinator should check by occasionally calling people at the outer tips of the tree to ensure they've been contacted. One of the largest citizens groups in the US, Common Cause, initiates most of its actions through an effective national telephone tree.

Community networks

Community-based computer networks – called community nets – have become important sources of local information. They provide free dial-up and web access, as well as community information, community discussions, expert advice, and e-mail. Most also provide web space and training on maintaining a website for local organizations.

E-mail newsletters

Another way of staying in touch with citizens locally and in other cities is through an e-mail newsletter To start an e-mail newsletter, put some interesting material on a website, then invite people to subscribe. You can bulk e-mail the newsletter to subscribers by entering their addresses as "Bcc" (blind cc) so that addresses remain invisible. The big advantage of e-mail newsletters is that you pay nothing for printing, distribution, and color photos.

The other way to do an e-mail newsletter is to put all the content on a website, then e-mail subscribers the web address. You can also build up a searchable archive on the site and hotlink to other interesting material. The main advantage of web delivery is that people without e-mail can view the newsletter at community centers and libraries with public web access.

Autodialer networks

For a few hundred dollars you can buy an autodialer that will send short messages to answering machines. The system uses a computer and database directory to digitize voice messages and then send them out automatically. Operating on one line, during weekdays, a single machine can deliver a one-minute message to 6,000 people per week. It's best to send messages to people who have said they wish to receive them and to send the messages during the day when they will reach answering machines or voice-mail.

A community group can also "cold call" people with bulletins or short messages they might reasonably assume people would want to receive. To obtain numbers for cold calling, buy a phone CD which contains millions of current names, addresses, and phone numbers that can be pulled off block by block. Because everyone gets their telephone messages, autodialers are useful for guaranteed delivery and for messages that have to go out quickly. They are useless for asking people to do something they would not normally do.

1.13 Fundraising

You do not need to fundraise to contribute to your community or take on a public interest project. However, you will probably need to fundraise to organize large numbers of people or launch a large public interest campaign. Because fundraising has many nasty side effects, the best option for small groups is to define an objective that is achievable without a lot of money.

Fundraising genetically alters organizations. They become less outspoken, more conservative, more inwardly focused, and more interested in pleasing foundation and government funders.

Charitable status helps fundraising, but it means abiding by government restrictions on political activity. The threat of losing the ability to issue tax receipts imposes a kind of self-censorship that suffocates edgy advocacy.

Another drawback of fundraising is that you usually have to spend money and time in order to raise money.

A small group with a single project may require very little outside money and should think twice about spending existing resources on fundraising projects with no guarantee of any return. Members can tap their own personal resources to provide meeting or office space, phone, fax, and volunteer time, or they can contribute their own funds to provide the small amount of money needed to cover the organization's maintenance costs (for administration, training/coordinating volunteers, basic inter-member communication). Most important, they can remain focused on their objective and avoid falling into the trap of building organization.

If you must raise money . . .

Ask frequently. Churches are some of the best fundraisers because they ask every week. Good fundraisers ask at every opportunity.

Ask publicly. Social pressure helps people part with their money. Again, the churches provide a model.

Ask personally. It is easier to toss a piece of direct mail than it is to refuse a real person.

Ask volunteers. They have already shown they want to help. Contributing financially strengthens their commitment.

Ask for amounts that will make a difference. Citizens groups have a habit of asking for far too little. They might charge $2 for membership rather than a useful $20. When raising money for a campaign, they aim for $1,000 instead of an effective $10,000.

Avoid events needing large amounts of up-front cash. Events that require expensive prizes can lose money.

Raise more money then you intend to spend. Extra money lets you address unforeseen difficulties, and exploit unforeseen opportunities.

Spend money to raise money. Consider hiring an experienced fundraiser or a staff person who can fundraise if there is no one in your group willing and able to raise money as a volunteer.

Fundraising sources

Individual contributions. Asking for contributions from local people turns fundraising into community building. People become more attached to groups, projects, and places they feel they own. Money can come from memberships, voluntary subscriptions to newsletters, collections at meetings, door-to-door canvassing, planned giving, memorial giving, and direct mail. There are many how-to books that cover these approaches.

In-kind donations. Seek in-kind or non-monetary contributions. This includes donations of printing, equipment, furniture, space, services, food, and time. Local businesses respond well to requests for in-kind donations.

Auctions. Elizabeth Amer recommends a dream auction in her book *Taking Action.* "Neighbors can donate overnight babysitting for two children, a local landmark embroidered on your jacket, cheesecake for eight, four hours of house repairs. At a big community party your auctioneer sells every treasure to the highest bidder."

Contests. The way to make money on a contest is to sell votes, one for 50 cents, a booklet for five dollars. Purchasers can use them to vote for their favorite entry in, for example, a garden contest or a contest for the best Christmas light display or the best-decorated Christmas tree. Contests can raise a lot of money as people try to stack the vote for their favorite. Winners usually get a prize.

Fundraising dinners. This standby succeeds if you charge a lot more than the dinner costs. It also helps to be able to keep what is earned on the bar. People come to fundraising dinners to help the cause and schmooze with other like-minded people.

Food tastings in local restaurants. This works well in places with lots of ethnic restaurants. People can purchase small tastes of many different kinds of food.

Casinos and bingos. In many places a registered non-profit society can make several thousand dollars a night by running a casino or a bingo. Typically a group will provide people to help staff the casino over several nights. Provincial and state gaming commissions provide applications and rules for gaming licenses.

Time tithing. In *When Everyone's a Volunteer,* Ivan Sheier recommends a system in which supporters contribute quality services as a way of producing a steady flow of cash. A group might advertise such member services as conducting a workshop, painting signs, or providing some form of professional assistance. When supporters perform a service, they do not keep the money they are paid, but have the amount, minus expenses, sent directly to their group.

Charging fees. Consider charging fees for services or products. Many social service non-profits contract with government to provide services to their constituents.

Bonding with rich elites. A collection of foundations financed by a tiny group of wealthy funders supplies the bulk of support for the environmental movement. If rich do-gooders find your objectives attractive, you might take the time to develop relationships with these people or the foundations that dispense their philanthropy.

Direct mail and telephone solicitation. Direct mail and telephone solicitation are such effective fundraising tools that most large social movement organizations use one or both. Small organizations should also consider these techniques because many communications companies that operate phone banks and produce direct mail charge a percentage of what they bring in. This means the group doesn't have to provide up-front money to pay the fundraiser, and it doesn't incur a debt if the fundraising appeal brings in next to nothing.

Grants from governments and foundations

If you have a particular project in mind, look for government programs that will provide funds. Many citizens groups are short of project money because they don't bother to find out about hundreds of existing government and foundation programs.

After identifying a possibility, find out about application procedures. Getting some grants requires writing a good proposal, but others only require filling in an application. Because there are so many programs from different governments and foundations, you can often fund a project with multiple grants.

HOW TO GET FOUNDATION FUNDING

Robert Bothwell, director and president of the National Committee of Responsive Philanthropy, conducted a study of 21 foundations and 26 grassroots organizations in the US to identify why foundation funding wasn't reaching grassroots organizations.

He followed the study with a series of recommendations, summarized here:

• Grassroots groups should market themselves more effectively. They need to use the media, tell their stories, and become publicly known for something important. This was the number one recommendation from foundations. Many grassroots groups ignore marketing, naively thinking they will become known by their good works alone.

• Grassroots organizations need to commit more resources to fundraising and increase their fundraising savvy.

• Grassroots groups should identify more foundation funding possibilities and submit more proposals. In the US, grassroots groups have a 63 percent success rate for proposals. The rule of thumb for professional fundraisers is a 10 to 17 percent success rate.

• Grassroots organizations should contact the foundations they identify as possible funders, do follow-up telephone calls and office visits, and generally seek to build relationships with foundation staff and trustees who seem interested in their work.

• Grassroots organizations should work in consortia and coalitions to amplify their work, visibility, and attractiveness to funders.

• Grassroots organizations with paid staff, or with mixed paid and volunteer staff, are much more likely to obtain foundation grants than organizations with just volunteer staff, or with no staff and a volunteer board of directors.

CHAPTER 2

Grassroots Relationships

T HIS CHAPTER LOOKS AT how to ensure healthy relationships among group members. Many action-oriented groups fall apart because they spend too much time developing actions and too little time developing good relationships.

2.1 Dialogue

Genuine dialogue is essential for healthy, productive human interaction, particularly when people get together to sort out a difficult issue. Here are some ways to promote dialogue.

Ensure the essentials for dialogue

Dialogue does not come naturally. You must be vigilant to ensure that three essentials are present:

Equality. Participants need to see one another as equals and try to eliminate the coercive influences of status and rank.

Empathetic listening. Participants need to respond with unreserved empathy to the views of others.

The expression of assumptions. Participants need to candidly examine and express their own often deep-rooted assumptions about an issue.

Substitute dialogue for debate

Instead of a you *or* me frame, try a you *and* me frame. Instead of trying to win, try to find common ground. Instead of critiquing other positions, reexamine all positions.

Adopt strategies for promoting dialogue

- Review what encourages and discourages dialogue.
- Include people who disagree.
- Initiate dialogue through a gesture of empathy.
- Focus on common interests, not divisive ones.
- Where appropriate, identify mistrust as the real problem.
- Encourage personal relationships to humanize transactions.

Learn to overcome habits that confound dialogue

Holding back and not participating. Go around the room and ask each person to talk about some personal experience related to the topic at hand.

Listening without hearing. Encourage listening to understand; discourage listening to find flaws. Ask participants to paraphrase what they think they heard the other person say.

Unexamined assumptions. Assumptions often box in the search for solutions. Reveal assumptions, but bring forth your own assumptions before speculating on those of others.

Old scripts. Expose scripts to a reality check. Old scripts are standard responses to difficult problems. An example of an old script is the idea that we should address drug addiction by hiring more police and by jailing users for longer periods of time.

Premature demands for action. Premature action precludes dialogue and can be counterproductive. Pause and ask the group whether more dialogue is needed.

Different starting points. It's difficult to reach consensus when people are at different stages of working through a problem. Consider the problem of "heroic" medicine, where enormous efforts are made to save a dying person at great financial and emotional cost. Those who have dealt with heroic efforts to keep a loved one alive will be "ahead" of most people who prefer not to think about the problem. In such cases you should provide issue books that spell out the consequences of choosing certain options. You should also allow extra time, if necessary, for people to work through emotional feelings about a difficult issue.

Showboating or grandstanding. Intervene if showboating goes on too long. Watch out for academics who may be less interested in dialogue than a display of how much they know.

Scoring debating points. Allow extra time to guide participants back to the rules of dialogue.

Pet preoccupations. Allow participants to express their preoccupations, and encourage others to show they understand the point even if they disagree. Well-intentioned leaders often block dialogue when they try to advance the interests of their constituents. This often takes the form of reiterating the pet preoccupations of various minorities, religious groups, the women's movement, the environmental movement, and others.

Separate decision making from dialogue. Don't mix exploring and creating options with decision making, which focuses on choosing from among options.

It is often helpful to have a trained facilitator and a preamble that sets forth the conditions for dialogue. These are necessary where there is an atmosphere of potential mistrust or where people with different backgrounds are trying to deal with contentious issues. For more information see Daniel Yankelovich's book *The Magic of Dialogue,* from which this section is derived.

2.2   Deep Community

In *The Different Drum: Community Making and Peace,* psychiatrist M. Scott Peck offers a different definition of the nature of real community and how it is created. He draws on his experience running workshops for the non-profit Institute for Community Encouragement, which aim at creating a deep level of connectedness between participants who have had no prior connection.

Peck believes any group can form itself into a community if it goes through three stages. In two-day workshops, Institute trainers take groups through these stages. In the first stage, *pseudocommunity*, everyone tries to be extremely pleasant and avoid disagreement. In the second stage, *chaos*, people argue and struggle in various ways to heal or convert one another. In the third stage, *emptiness*, people stop acting like they have it all together and begin to share their own defeats, failures, sins, and inadequacies. According to Peck, if a group can move through *emptiness*, it can achieve community.

Community is characterized by realism, humility, self-awareness, and the inclusion of people who are different. Once a group achieves community, the most frequent comment is: "I feel safe here." Peck notes that the usual way out of *chaos* is organization.

He argues that excessive organization and strong leaders are a threat to community. Keep in mind that Peck is mainly interested in forming deep bonds between people. Because activists are mainly interested in getting things done, they have to give organization and leadership some consideration.

2.3 Wrangling Reduction

Wrangling, confusion, and going in circles drive people nuts. They get frustrated when *they* can see what should be done, but no one else seems to understand. Here are some ways to reduce wrangling.

Make sure everyone starts with the same facts. The Japanese claim that when everyone has the same facts, the way to proceed is obvious to everyone. Take the time to make sure everyone has the same information. For more see 3.2 "Researching a project."

Don't mix creating options with deciding among options. Creating options requires people to be uncritical. Deciding among options requires people to be just the opposite. For more on community problem solving see 3.3 "Planning a Project."

Bypass fixations when creating options. Fixating on a single approach can truncate the search for alternatives. If someone fixates, record his/her idea with an assurance it will be considered later.

Assign the role of grease. To avoid process problems, assign someone with facilitation skills to act as grease at each meeting. Ideally, everyone in your group will have facilitation skills and can take over this role. Facilitators not only keep discussion moving, but they also sometimes stop it to provide a chance to talk about how the discussion is going or how people are relating to one another. This kind of meta-language (talk about talk) is a time-out to resolve hidden assumptions, concerns, or irritations that are preventing the group from moving forward. For more see 1.11 "Facilitating."

2.4 Mediation and Conflict Resolution

Mediation skills may be unnecessary for small groups composed of people who enjoy one another's company. But these skills may be needed for large groups containing many different points of view. The best guide to conflict resolution is *Getting to Yes* by Roger Fisher and William Ury. The following covers the bare essentials of *Getting to Yes*.

Prohibit personal attacks. Agree to focus on the problem instead of the person. Chairs and facilitators should intervene at the first hint of personal attack. Nothing proceeds when a substantive problem becomes entangled with an unhealthy relationship. In some cases attacks arise from nothing more than another person resembling a mother, a father, or an ex-spouse.

When the possibility of personal attacks arises, the chairperson can ask everyone to avoid the word "you" and express views in the first person "I." Thus a participant might say, "I feel my proposal should have been taken seriously," instead of "You always make fun of my proposals."

Consider a listening exercise. Unresolved conflicts drive people away. When rivalries, intolerances, or conflicts arise between individuals, take time to resolve them. A simple listening exercise developed by the Quakers often works. Under the guidance of a listening referee, each person states his/her views while the other listens; then the other person givers an interpretation of what he/she has heard. This is repeated until each person agrees on the other's interpretation. The two parties then try to resolve their differences.

Focus on interests, not positions. This is the most important recommendation in *Getting to Yes*. Focusing on interests allows movement because in most cases an interest (need, desire, concern) can be satisfied by a number of different positions. Begin by acknowledging the interests of others.

Separate the people from the problem. Speak about yourself, not about them. Look forward, not back. If there is a people problem, deal with it directly by speaking about perceptions. Take the time to turn strangers into people you know. Make symbolic gestures (shaking hands or an embrace, a thank-you card, an invitation to lunch) to improve shaky relationships.

Invent options for mutual gain. To invent options for mutual gain, switch off your critical voice and create ideas that will work for everybody. Conflict resolution really begins to work when people start thinking of themselves as being on the same side.

Insist on using objective criteria. Many negotiations become a battle of wills. To avoid this, frame each issue as a *joint* search for objective criteria that will decide the outcome of the negotiation. Objective criteria include fair standards such as market value, precedent, equal treatment, court rulings, and efficiency. They also include fair practices. Remember the fair way to divide a piece of cake between two children: One cuts, the other chooses.

AFFINITY GROUPS, ZAPS, AND ACTIONS

In *Lessons from the Damned*, Nancy E. Stoller describes the practices of ACT-UP. The most interesting are those that side-step the chore of getting everyone to agree on a single course of action. They permit people with minority views to pursue different actions and still remain connected to the larger group.

"ACT-UP formed to address the AIDS crisis through direct action. Its success comes from its ability to accommodate people with different political agendas and different time commitments. Numerous ACT-UP groups across the country hold meetings every Monday night. They follow a standard two-hour format that begins with co-facilitators, one male and one female, leading the audience in a recital of ACT-UP's two-line statement of purpose that ends with: "We are not silent." Applause follows. New members are asked to stand up. They are applauded and handed a sign-in sheet by someone assigned responsibility for them. Following these bonding rit-uals, people come to the front to give committee reports and announcements in groups of five. Next come proposals for zaps and actions. Zaps are actions that can be organized in a week. Actions are more elaborate and may involve media and organizing work spread over months. After members hear and vote on all proposals, those who wish to work on one of them leave the room to plan. This direct voting with your feet quickly identifies the resources available for each zap or action."

"Although each zap or action needs to be approved by con-sensus at a Monday meeting, an affinity group can still pursue those that are not. Affinity groups frequently pull off panned projects to everyone's satisfaction. A graphics committee pro-posed the famous silence=death logo at a meeting and encountered objections. So they formed an affinity group and went off, got the logo printed on T-shirts, then came back to the group. Everybody said: It's fabulous; it's great. Silence=death then became the logo for the organization."

Progressive cities provide mediators. Nasty problems and community battles involving many people require professional mediators. Progressive cities such as Portland, Oregon, have mediators on staff to help residents resolve problems.

2.5   Group Structure

Less is more

A small citizens group should have as little structure as possible. The right amount is just enough to achieve an immediate goal. In an attempt to become legitimate, many groups decide they need more structure. Unfortunately, this can lead to spending more time on the needs of the organization and losing sight of the reason for getting together in the first place.

Larger projects require more organization and staff

Small all-volunteer groups can handle short-term projects that do not require large outlays of money. The need for organization increases with the number of projects, the size of projects, the number of people involved, and the amount of dedicated time needed to manage the organization and carry out projects.

Signs that suggest the need for more paid staff.

- Burned-out volunteers.
- Too much work.
- Too little accomplished.
- Fundraising failures. (Funders may need someone responsible before they will give money to an organization.)
- Too few partners. (Businesses, non-profits, government departments, and schools will work with funded organizations. Flat all-volunteer groups make them nervous.)
- Little respect from the press. (The media view organizations as easier to reach and more reliable than volunteer groups.)

Small all-volunteer groups can easily get into trouble if members assume someone else will regularly take responsibility for mailing out information, managing databases, answering letters, meeting with government officials, contacting other groups with similar interests, writing grant applications, and a host of other routine activities. This kind of work usually requires at least one paid staff person. Most informal groups move toward more organization by forming a non-profit society, electing a board, applying for grants, then hiring a coordinator.

Both large and small groups should strive for leanness to maintain a focus on mission. This means they should:

- keep organization to a minimum,
- keep the staff to a minimum (a coordinator may be all that is necessary),
- keep expenses to a minimum (in, small lean organizations the coordinator may operate out of a spare room in his/her own home), and
- keep the board size to a minimum.

To sustain an organization, build in a paid position that will continue to exist only if the organization continues to do its work. If more paid work needs to be done, consider hiring people on contract or providing an honorarium.

If you must hire staff, hire a great coordinator

If there is too much work for an all-volunteer group, you may have to hire a coordinator. Look for a person who is energetic, capable of figuring out what is required, then acting. A great coordinator will be willing and able to approach many different individuals, groups, and organizations to drive a project forward. Examine the most effective non-profits and you will find at the center a dynamic leader in the role of coordinator.

Be careful of traditional structure

Traditional structure seems to focus too much on organization for most small all-volunteer groups. Nevertheless, it continues to be recommended for larger citizens groups. The most successful have the following elements:

- An elected leadership. Some groups elect officers – a president, one or two vice-presidents, a secretary, and a treasurer. In order to include people doing important work, some expand the leadership group into a steering committee that includes the chairperson of each committee.
- Regular meetings
- A newsletter
- A means of delegating tasks and responsibilities
- Training for new members

- Social time together
- A planning process
- A way of training, managing, and rewarding volunteers
- Working relationships with power players and resource organizations (Power players are people with the ability to make things happen: politicians, owners of key businesses, media people, heads of key government departments, heads of agencies, major landlords.)

Be careful of non-profit status

In Canada, traditional organizations frequently wind up as registered non-profit societies. There are few advantages to non-profit status beyond less circuitous access to certain sources of funds. On the other hand, non-profit status means having to follow the rules and the organizational structure required by law.

Committees and task forces

In larger organizations, committees and task forces are the main way jobs are shared. They make it possible to get a lot done without anyone getting worn out. Standing committees look after a continuing group function; task forces carry out a specific task, then disband. Both provide members with a way of getting involved in projects that interest them. A large, action-oriented group might have standing committees for coordinating actions, publicity, membership, outreach, newsletter, fundraising, and research. Many people prefer working on a short-term task force instead of a standing committee.

Ideally, committees and task forces are made up of people selected by the whole group rather than by people who are self-selected. If the whole group is confident in a task force or committee, it should empower the subgroup to make decisions on its own. To keep everyone working together, committees and task forces should regularly report back to the whole group. For more on volunteer work see *When Everyone's a Volunteer* by Ivan Sheier.

Networks

Many grassroots organizations work well as flat, informal networks with no executive or board of directors. Flatness, or the absence of an organizational hierarchy, does not necessarily mean the elimination of individual roles or responsibilities. It does mean an end to people with overriding authority over other people's work.

Unlike formal organizations, networks grow or shrink depending on the energy of participants, available resources, and external circumstances. Some ad hoc networks grow very large very quickly, then suddenly disappear. Many citizens groups suffer from involving small numbers of people heavily. Networks thrive on involving large numbers of people lightly.

The degree and style of organization are important issues for every group. To make the right choices you will need to be clear about your objectives, your ability to raise resources, and the way members wish to relate to one another.

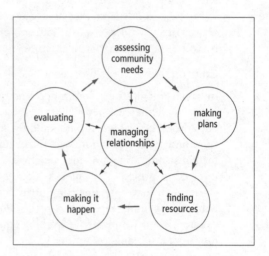

Health Canada's diagram of community action.
Action is treated as a step-by-step sequence

CHAPTER

3

Designing and Running a Project

DESIGNING AND CARRYING OUT community projects is an integral part of community organizing and development. The focus in this chapter is on place-based projects where citizens work together to provide a public good or community benefit.

Your group may wish to pursue a more difficult project, one that faces opposition from people in power. For this kind of project you will need to be able to negotiate, campaign, and agitate. The material in this chapter will help, but you will also want to read the chapters on strategic thinking, direct contact, and media advocacy.

3.1 Real Projects Make Messy Diagrams

Place-based citizen action is often presented as a step-by-step sequence, as in the diagram from Health Canada opposite. The ingredients of a process often make sense, but the step-by-step sequence usually fails to fit actual circumstances.

Instead of a sequence, look at ingredients. Which of these you focus on at any given time will depend on what is actually happening at the moment. Add or repeat ingredients based on an assessment of what is missing or needed. And keep in mind that the various ingredients of community action are interwoven and interdependent. For example, planning requires research, which depends on getting and keeping people, which is affected by decision making, which requires evaluating, and so on.

3.2 Researching a Project

Research before reacting

Let's suppose your focus is a neighborhood problem in a city. Cities behave in tricky ways. What may seem an obvious solution often appears less so after a little research. Acting before researching can waste a lot of time, and it can reinforce the stereotype of active citizens as highly vocal, but largely uninformed. The stereotype is the most often cited excuse for dismissing calls for greater citizen participation in local decision making.

Here is a typical story of what can happen for lack of a little research. People living in a quiet neighborhood receive notice of a proposal to use a nearby residence as a psychiatric halfway house. Fears of "crazy people" running amok prompt them to form an ad hoc citizens group, which moves swiftly into action to combat the proposal. Having skipped research, they don't discover that most special needs residential facilities (or SNRFs) do not create problems or reduce property values. They don't discover that most local residents are not even aware of SNRFs in their neighborhood. Without these facts, the group goes to battle. Over nothing.

Gather existing information

If your focus is a local issue, your municipal planning department may be able to help. It will usually have community profiles, traffic studies, zoning and other maps, aerial photos, and possibly an official community plan. Local health authorities or service agencies may have a needs assessment or more focused social studies of your area. Back copies of community newsletters and local newspapers will contain the recent history of many local issues. Your branch of the public library will have copies of many local reports, studies and newsletters.

Find out what people want

In the absence of a single overriding concern, a neighborhood group will have to identify what people feel is important. In many cases you will have to answer the following questions:

- What do residents like about the neighborhood, and what do they want to change?
- What are the opportunities for making the neighborhood more interesting, identifiable, helpful, friendly?
- What is the highest priority problem? Who is affected?

- Where is it located? What has been done? What can be done? Who can help?

Give this research some time. It can take a group a couple of evenings to itemize, condense, and prioritize responses to a question such as "What do you like about the neighborhood, and what do you want to change?" The following are two methods you can use to address difficult questions.

Consider a survey. Many activists mistakenly believe what concerns them will concern everybody. Only a survey will say for sure. A survey requiring face-to-face interaction not only provides useful information, but also helps build community.

Go to those in the know. Interview those who know what is going on in the community, and those who know how to deal with an issue. Often they are people with first-hand experience. A small focus-group discussion with six teens can reveal more about teens than a survey of 500 adults.

Discover your human resources

To really understand your neighborhood, you need to research its capacity to act. Start by answering these questions:

- Who can help?
- What resources does the community have (i.e., churches, hospitals, schools, business groups, religious organizations, citizen associations, clubs, ethnic groups, sports and recreational groups, cultural associations, service groups, major property owners, businesses, individuals)? For a practical guide to tapping local capacity by working in partnership with other organizations see John Kretzmann and John McKnight's book *Building Communities from the Inside Out*.
- How, why, and where do people get together?
- How do people find out what is going on?
- Who has a stake in the neighborhood?
- Who most influences local decisions, local funding, and local investment?

Research solutions from other places

Your problem may seem unique, but people in other places have probably faced similar problems. Rather than start from scratch, you can save a lot of time by finding out how they have addressed the problem. Start locally with other neighborhoods by contacting neighborhood associations – most towns and cities try to keep an up-to-date list. Then move on to other cities. For place-based problem solving in the US contact the National Civic League, or look up back issues of its journal, the *National Civic Review*. In Canada the Federation of Canadian Municipalities might be able to help.

3.3   Planning a Project

Planning is necessary if you want to avoid wasted activity and make your collective efforts count. Planning should move from the general to the specific, from the big picture to the small, from the long term to the short, from "what" to "how." It entails:

- setting an objective,
- devising strategies to achieve the objective, and
- devising actions to carry out the strategies.

For more information, see Chapter 7 on strategic action.

Look beyond the obvious to find good objectives

So often people assume it's obvious what needs to be done. Let's suppose the problem is mounting juvenile crime. It's obvious the neighborhood should try to get more policing, right? Well maybe, but there might be better or easier objectives. For instance, if you looked beyond symptoms at causes, you might decide to try to open local schools during evenings for youth activities. Research can help you look beyond the obvious.

How do your objectives score?

Create ideas for objectives that will lead to your goal, and then decide which to pursue. Test alternative objectives by asking:

- Will it improve people's lives or confer a public good?
- Is it easy to understand?
- Is it specific?
- Will you know when you've reached your objective?
- Will it have an immediate impact?
- Will it contribute to reaching long-term goals?
- Will other citizens want to help?
- Will it establish healthy connections between people?

- Is it attainable?
- Is it attainable with available resources?

For projects that face opposition, add the following questions:

- Is there a clear decision maker who can deliver the goods?
- Is it attractive enough to raise money?
- Is it deeply felt?
- Will it help to build organizing skills?
- Will it give citizens a sense of their own power?
- Is there a basic principle involved?

One objective at a time

To be effective, a small group should pursue only one objective at a time. A new group should begin with a short-term project with a high probability of success.

One good way to identify a group's priorities is to ask each person to write his or her priorities on large post-it notes, one priority per note. Each person then sticks their notes on a large sheet of paper where everyone can see them. Finally, a facilitator helps the group arrange the notes into clusters with similar characteristics. The top priority soon becomes apparent.

Map the landscape of support and opposition

One of the most important recurring decisions for any group is what their strategy will be in the face of opposition. Given the situation at hand, what is going to be most effective: cooperation, negotiation, or confrontation? Smart groups do not have a single style; they constantly respond to shifting circumstances by deciding what is most appropriate at the moment.

Generally they make every attempt to succeed through cooperation and negotiation, reserving confrontation for clear and continuing intransigence.

As you think about strategy, you will need to answer the following questions:

- Where can you find the resources you need? Who will support your initiative? What concerns will they have? How can you take advantage of their support?
- Who will oppose your initiative? What concerns will they have? What form will their opposition take?

Design the action

Once you know what you want to achieve, brainstorm ideas for actions that will get you there. Consider a brainstorming session with allies; this will improve the chances they will take part in carrying out actions. Devising your own action will be more fun and the result will probably be more effective. Ordinary people can be very creative if given a few hours to invent interesting alternatives to the usual actions expected of citizens groups. New ideas don't have to be completely new; you might significantly vary a familiar action that has become stale and ineffective.

If you are unfamiliar with brainstorming, follow the advice of a guide like Charles Thompson's *What a Great Idea*. Before beginning, participants should agree to fool around, avoid criticizing, go for lots of ideas, and build on one another's suggestions.

Choosing an action

After you have a good collection of action alternatives, you can evaluate them and decide which to carry forward. A good way to evaluate a collection of action possibilities is to do a quick cost-benefit analysis of each. Costs should include required money, time, and numbers of people. Benefits should include the degree to which the action furthers an objective, helps build group morale, and helps to facilitate other actions. Most benefits should be assessed according to the probability of success. If the action is intended mainly to increase morale but only has a 50 percent chance of succeeding, then the probability of *reducing* morale because of failure is also 50 percent.

TASK	thinking	options	feel	role	messed up by
CREATE		increase	😊	child	your internal voice of judgement
JUDGE		decrease	😐	parent	a tendency to protect your ideas

Creating and judging require very different kinds of thinking. Don't mix them.

Planning the action

Once your group agrees on an action, create an action plan. It should include the following elements:

- a time frame

- an action coordinator

- an ordered list of tasks to complete

- names of persons responsible for each task

- required resources, including materials, facilities and funds

Keep action plans flexible so you can respond to the unexpected.

3.4   Carrying Out a Project

Once you've completed the necessary groundwork, you need to act. Surprisingly, many groups never get around to acting. John Gardner, author of *On Leadership* and cofounder of Common Cause, says, "Many talk about action but are essentially organized for study, discussion or education. Still others keep members busy with organizational housekeeping, committee chores, internal politics and passing of resolutions."

While many interest groups get together just for discussion, community groups tend to work best when acting accompanies talking. Otherwise they tend to shrink to a few diehards for whom meeting attendance has become a way of life.

Long-term projects require steps and cheerleaders

Some small actions, like planting a tree, may be complete in themselves. Other actions may be part of a series designed to achieve an objective over many years. These kinds of actions are more difficult to pull off because people give up and drop out.

Long-term projects should be organized into small steps so participants feel they are getting somewhere.

Long-term projects require constant efforts to keep spirits up, and constant reminders to keep applying pressure. Good organizers know that most decision makers will eventually give in, if the group perseveres and continues to apply pressure. For more on winning by persevering see 6.10 "Grassroots Wilt 10: The catch-22 of collective action."

3.5   Publicizing a Project

Publicizing a project usually means working with the media to inform a wider public of what you are doing. Publicity can also buoy up participants, bring in more volunteers, nudge bureaucrats, unhinge politicians, and add momentum to a grassroots initiative. According to David Engwicht in *Reclaiming Our Cities and Towns*, empowerment comes from simple exposure. "Group members say, 'Did you see we were in the news again. Isn't it great? We are really starting to get places now.'"

When you understand the media, you can also raise public issues that are being ignored and reframe issues from a citizen's perspective (see Appendix 3). Be careful, however, if you are not used to dealing with the media. Many journalists look for stories rooted in conflict, error, and injustice. They may impose a confrontational agenda that can actually make it more difficult for you to resolve your issue.

Some media basics are briefly covered below, but you may need more help with this important subject. If so, see Chapter 9 on media advocacy.

Assemble a list of sympathetic journalists. If you have a positive community story, you may have trouble getting a reporter interested. One way around this is to cultivate a list of journalists who care about community building. Note their deadlines so you can call when the pressure is off.

Find the media professionals in your community. Seek help from the people in your community who work for newspapers, radio, and television stations. They can provide advice on what is newsworthy, how to get attention, and who to call. Most will not want to appear in the foreground, but in the background they will be invaluable.

Define your messages, then create your quotes. Don't rush off to the media without a clear idea of what you want to accomplish. Create one or two messages. Messages are what you want people to remember. If you intend to air a problem, one of your messages should be a reasonable solution. Once you have your messages figured out, you need to turn them into quotable quotes. For more on messages and quotes see Chapter 9.

Make actions newsworthy. To get media attention you need to tell a good story, with a human focus, about something that is happening now. The more creative, colorful, and humorous the story, the better coverage will be. Getting noticed is largely a matter of dramatizing issues.

Look for timing opportunities. Try to link your issue to breaking news or to a government report, an anniversary, or a special holiday. Linking helps to make old issues current. Good timing is the key to getting publicity.

Write letters to the editor. An easy way to get publicity is to write a letter to the editor of your local community newspaper. Small papers will publish any reasonable letter that does not require a lot of fact checking. Draft and redraft letters so they are punchy and short. Check the length so your letter is at least as short as the average published letter. Letters to the editor are also one of the most effective ways of influencing politicians.

Issue media advisories. Send out a media advisory on your group's letterhead if you have an upcoming event you wish to publicize. At the top left put "Media Advisory" and the date. Next, create a strong newspaper-style headline that will interest an editor who has to shuffle through hundreds of media advisories and news releases every day. The first sentence of the copy should contain the most important or most interesting fact in your story. The rest of the release should cover the essentials of who, what, where, when, and why. At the bottom put "For more information" and a contact name and phone number. Keep it to one page long.

For big events, fax out a media advisory two days prior, then telephone to make sure it was received and noticed. Direct it to the assignment desk for TV, to the city desk for newspapers, and to the newsroom for radio. Better still direct it to an actual person. Faxing an advisory without any personal contact is usually a waste of time unless you are sending it to small newspapers.

The best way to get the press to an event is to phone assignment editors, producers, and reporters one or two days in advance.

If no one comes to cover your event, phone around and offer a news release and interviews after it is over.

Aim at TV. Some of the most effective citizens groups get TV coverage by staging events that provide action and good pictures. Greenpeace, for instance, gets attention by sending little rubber boats out to buzz around huge aircraft carriers. Consider interviews at the location of the story. Use large colorful graphs and maps, or arrange to provide graphic evidence. Some groups also shoot their own broadcast-quality video or create video news releases to help control what is broadcast.

Try to schedule actions before three o'clock to allow reporters enough time to process material for the six o'clock news. Choose a spokesperson who comes across well on TV, where a great deal is communicated non-verbally through tone of voice, facial expression, and body gestures.

Practice your blurb. TV and radio news editors often cut quotes so they take only 15 to 30 seconds. Make sure you give reporters 15 to 30 second sound bites that carry your message. Don't say anything that would misrepresent your message if it was taken out of context. Practice what you want to say before the event. Your statement or a minor variation can be used in response to any question asked. No one will know the difference.

Reframe stories on live radio. If you can get on a live radio show, you can actually shape the news because you won't be edited as you would be on TV or in the newspaper. Prepare a collection of quotable quotes that convey your message. Write them out and take them with you to the interview.

Don't rely on the media to educate. The mass media are good at entertaining and good at raising issues, but poor at providing detailed information that would help people understand issues. If you want to circulate detailed information, you will probably have to do it through newsletters, op-ed page features, projects with schools, conferences, workshops, and websites.

Consider other kinds of announcements. You can announce your event on radio and cable TV "bulletin boards", and in event guides published by community newspapers. The ethnic media is another outlet that is often overlooked.

You might also consider a public service announcement. These are public interest "ads" aired by radio and TV for free or a reduced rate. Call to find out local media's PSA guidelines; they usually rule out PSAs that are "political." For radio, send in public service announcements of 30 seconds or about 75 words. Include start and stop dates for running the ad, plus information on your organization.

Consider other media. Promote your event or issue in a leaflet delivered by volunteers, by ad mail, or by direct mail. Leafleting can be combined with fundraising that will pay for the leaflet, the distribution, and project administration.

You can also display messages on printed T-shirts, buttons, window signs, roof-rack car signs, stick-on car signs, posters, free postcards, slides shown before movies in movie theaters, brochures in the public library, bumper stickers, notices in apartment building laundries, church orders of service, and the newsletters of other groups. For more methods see 1.5 "Getting More People" and 1.12 "Information Sharing."

Try the direct approach. Consider phoning or writing those who have the power to put things right. If you have a city-related problem that you cannot solve, even with the help of city staff, try the direct approach and call a city councilor.

3.6   Evaluating a Project

Your group will need to evaluate both projects and processes if you wish to improve your effectiveness and stay on track. Unfortunately, most grassroots groups rarely evaluate either.

Make evaluation part of your group's culture

Make a habit of asking what worked and what could be better for both actions and projects. Consider using a round to evaluate group process at the end of meetings.

If you don't ask for honest feedback, you won't get it. Unhappy people will simply drop out. To get the most honest feedback, ensure anonymous responses and obtain responses from people outside your immediate group.

Check on benefits to members. After an action, ask participants about benefits. Did they learn anything? Did they have too little or too much to do? Did they have any fun? Did they feel part of the group?

The Industrial Areas Foundation (Appendix 1) treats actions as opportunities to develop leaders. Organizers sit down with individual leaders and go through a detailed examination of what happened and why. The emphasis is on self-discovery and personal growth. Organizers challenge leaders to examine personal obstacles, and to work out a plan to overcome them.

Compare results with objectives. Is there a gap between what is happening and what you want to happen? If there is a persistent gap, you might consider getting help from a professional organizer. Another way of dealing with a persistent gap is to revise your objectives.

YOU ARE INVITED TO
A BLACK BIRTHDAY PARTY TO
CELEBRATE THE 100TH YEAR OF
THE MITCHELL HOUSE

Sunday, May 2
1:00 pm - 1:30 pm
12th & Fraser on the Street

On its 100th anniversary the Mitchell House has been largely destroyed by two arson attacks.

The birthday party will protest the lack of adequate protection for Vancouver's heritage buildings.

Several guests will speak on heritage preservation, the large number of heritage buildings lost to fires, and the need for the City to take steps to prevent the best buildings in Vancouver from being burned to ashes.

Dress in Black
Bring a Black umbrella if it's raining
Black birthday cake will be served

EAST MOUNT PLEASANT RESTORATION COMMITTEE

This leaflet delivered door to door helped to organize a neighborhood. Many people attended the Black Birthday Party held to commemorate the 100th birthday of a house destroyed by arson.

C H A P T E R 4

Projects that
Bring People Together

THIS CHAPTER OUTLINES a collection of neighborhood projects that introduce people to one another. These projects help to create a sense of social place. They help to extend the sense of neighborhood beyond buildings and streets to the people who live there. These projects provide a basis for daily congeniality and for getting together to address local issues. However, because they are brief and require no ongoing contact amongst participants, they do not contribute substantially to the social life of a community. This requires the kind of community building *practices* outlined in Chapter 5.

4.1 Community Protection

Block cleanups

A simple litter cleanup can provide an opportunity for everyone on a block to meet one another. In many small towns, one-day neighborhood cleanups involving adults, kids, and a variety of civic officials have become a recognized way of building community and instilling pride in place.

Cleanups aimed at removing major junk require partners and more planning. Local governments will often supply trucks to haul away the products of big cleanups; local businesses might contribute dumpster bins. Cleaning up your block can include graffiti removal, weeding, fence painting, and hedge trimming. It can also extend to helping those on your block who lack the strength or resources to maintain their own property.

Block Watch

One of the most formal community-building activities is a police-sponsored Block Watch program. Block Watch attempts to reduce crime by encouraging people to keep an eye on the street and their neighbors' property, and to report any suspicious activity to 911.

Typically a block is organized across the rear lane, since most forced entries into buildings occur from the rear. Each Block Watch has a captain and a co-captain, who undergo a police security check and then receive an identification badge. Block captains usually set up an initial organizing meeting to introduce neighbors to one another. A volunteer draws up a map of the block with names and phone numbers, and supplies copies to the police and other members of the Watch. Police officers will attend the meeting, if requested, to talk about local policing issues and ways of securing your home.

In many cases, Block Watch leads to other block activities, from block cleanups and pet minding to plant swapping. When neighbors get together they find they have more in common than an interest in security.

Evaluations of Block Watch programs indicate they reduce crime when neighbors know one another. Cop-driven efforts with little resident involvement contribute little to security or a sense of community.

Block Parents

A Block Parent program is another initiative often sponsored by the police. Police typically run security checks on potential candidates as they do with Block Watch captains. Block Parents provide a safe haven for children and, occasionally, seniors. When Block Parents are available to answer the door, they post a sign in their window. In an emergency, children who find themselves in trouble can turn to a Block Parent house for assistance.

Community crime prevention

Taking part in community crime prevention is a way to meet your neighbors and help make your community a safer place to live. Organized citizen participation in crime prevention usually begins with the opening of a community crime prevention office where people can meet with one another and the police to address local concerns. The activities of an office staffed largely by volunteers include meeting and talking with locals, running crime prevention programs, referring people to various agencies, sharing community information, conducting workshops, operating foot patrols, and organizing other local projects.

The premise behind community crime prevention is that police need to do more than react to incidents. They can be more effective if they spend time on public awareness, partnerships with citizens, and local problem solving. A common weakness of community crime prevention is too much police and not enough community.

Heritage home guard

Large numbers of heritage and other buildings have burned down because they have been left vacant. Homeless people and drug users move into empty buildings and set fires accidentally; delinquents or arsonists target empty buildings and set fires deliberately. Empty buildings are so vulnerable that insurance contracts usually include a clause that allows insurance companies to avoid paying on a claim if an owner fails to inform them when a building is vacated. Boarding up the building helps a little, on the other hand it identifies the building as empty and an easy target.

The best way to protect any building is to solicit the help of neighbors. Battery-powered trips and sensors can be wired to turn on battery-powered electric flares mounted in the widows on a side of the building observed by a neighbor. Flashing lights are the signal to call in the authorities. Trips or sensors can also be wired to switch on a wireless intercom, walkie-talkie, or baby monitor with a receiver in a neighbor's house. Alternatively, one can adapt many of the small, inexpensive, burglar alarm gizmos available at hardware stores. Simple technology coupled with monitoring by neighbors could save a lot of buildings and, in the process, introduce a lot of people to one another.

Urban Signaling

Crime and urban decay increase in neighborhoods that signal crime and urban decay have already begun to set in. A downward spiral begins as criminals and drug dealers move in and families and businesses move out. The opposite process happens when there are signals that residents care about the neighborhood. Well-kept yards, well-maintained buildings, and clean streets attract families and businesses, and the neighborhood gets a reputation for being a good place to live.

Urban signaling is an interesting phenomenon because it suggests that appearances trigger a process that converts inferences into reality. A few derelict buildings may have nothing to do with the onset of decline, but they can hint at decline. And this hint can alter people's behavior, turning an isolated suggestion into a widespread fact. The consequence of small matters of appearance is so pronounced that community groups have learned it is wise to address "broken window syndrome" by quickly eliminating the signals of neglect.

Community groups can erase signals of decline as soon as they appear by forming partnerships with businesses, schools, and local government. They can fix broken windows, paint out graffiti, remove junk, and mow overgrown yards. In the process they will build community networks that will make further improvement easier as more people get involved.

4.2   Environmental Projects

There are so many possibilities for community-based environmental activities they could fill an entire book. Here are a few.

In situ awareness projects

Children and adults stencil yellow salmon next to catch-basins in a number of Pacific seaboard cities to remind people that what we put into our storm sewers eventually ends up in our oceans. Government-supported programs encourage people to paint the salmon by providing a kit containing a video, instruction manual, latex paint and template, and a reflective vest, as well as leaflets to distribute throughout the neighborhood. The project works well when school kids to do the stencilling as part of a science class.

Stream restoration projects

Salmon stream restoration is one of the most popular projects on the West Coast. Local volunteers clear clogged streams of debris and replant the banks with native species. Sometimes projects focus on creating a new salmon stream where none ever existed; some carve a new stream through a built-up area, with careful attention to avoiding toxic runoff from streets. Governments often participate in these projects by providing funding and the fry that will eventually return to the stream to spawn.

Bird habitat projects

Bird habitat projects focus on restoring local habitat to bring back birds that have disappeared from an area. A project might include planting native seed-bearing plants in parks and lanes, or building birdhouses to attract a particular species. Bird habitat projects are good venues for bringing kids, parents, and community activists together.

Community gardens

Community gardens are parcels of land divided into small plots in which local residents grow their own flowers, fruit, and vegetables. Community gardens owe their existence to the energy of residents. Some began as Victory Gardens during World War II; others were started by apartment dwellers who decided to cultivate an unused municipal lot or a railway right-of-way.

Finding a site for a municipally approved garden can be a long search. Once the garden is in place, there is always a waiting list of people who want to join. Typically, plots range from full size (100 to 120 square feet) to half size and rent for approximately $10 to $20 a year. Gardeners share common space, fertilizer, tools, a toolshed, and sometimes the cost of buying plants. Other expenses include the cost of metered water and public liability insurance. Gardeners meet several times over the growing season: once for a formal start-up, then a few times over the summer for informal potluck dinners and an annual open house.

Guerrilla gardening

Residents of many city neighborhoods have turned into insurgent Johnny Appleseeds. They have been quietly adding berries, vegetables, self-seeding annuals, and long-blooming perennials to lanes, boulevards, and traffic circles.

Unpaved back lanes are ideal targets for guerrilla gardening. Some people reintroduce native plants; others have food plants and flowers. In Vancouver, one woman takes the seed heads from her large pink poppies and sprinkles them up and down the alley, to great effect the following year.

Guerrilla gardening provides an easy first step beyond private property into the public realm. Guerrilla gardeners begin to see public space as something they, rather than government, are responsible for. They also begin to see that many public improvements only happen through citizen initiative.

Guerrilla gardening is wholesome mischief. It breaks the law but improves public property. Because its wholesomeness is clearly apparent, some cities have started to institutionalize it with programs that invite local residents to "adopt" and plant traffic circles, boulevards, and other pieces of public property.

Gleaning projects

In traditional communities, harvesting was an activity that brought everyone together. In modern cities a version of this has reappeared in the form of cooperative gleaning, usually focused on the harvesting of fruit that would otherwise be left to rot. Here is the way organizers describe the Vancouver Fruit Tree Project:

> *Our idea is simple: we build communities and strengthen food security using local backyard fruit. We connect people who have excess fruit from their backyard fruit trees with those who have the time and energy to harvest it. Most of the harvested fruit is donated to community organizations and individuals in need. We also offer canning and pruning workshops to pass on skills which are quickly being lost.*

People become involved as volunteers who contribute to picking fruit, distributing fruit, or training people to care for fruit trees. Others become involved as donors of backyard fruit. Still others contribute tripod ladders, pruning gear, and canning equipment. Harvesting projects can go awry if they focus too heavily on the quantity of food gathered. The best projects focus on having fun and doing something productive with others who live nearby.

4.3   Community Image-making

A distinctive appearance helps to define a neighborhood. Large brick buildings with tall windows and large cornices often indicate a historic town center. Bedragoned lampposts, open-air markets, ornate buildings, and distinctive signage define a Chinatown. Sometimes there is nothing that expresses the past or present identity of a neighborhood. For this reason, many communities decide to add banners, cairns, signs, flags, clocks, and gates that say who they are. These elements should have a real connection to the place; they should not be generic junk or themed paste-ons.

This section will focus on image-making that requires direct citizen involvement. It is one of the best ways to bring together diverse social and ethnic groups.

Signs name and define neighborhood boundaries

Progressive cities like Seattle have helped residents name their neighborhoods and then helped them design and install colorful street signs to mark the boundaries. In less progressive cities, citizens may have to undertake a naming project on their own

Resident-defined neighborhoods are small and numerous (a city of 500,000 will usually end up with 120), and they often overlap, so the boundary of one may be inside the boundary of another.

Once you have identified the boundaries, invite residents to take part in the naming their neighborhood. Names can come from historic references such as the names of old creeks, farms that once covered the area, early residents, early businesses, interesting events. Names can also come from natural or landscape features, or from prominent landmarks.

When you have settled on the name, identify a graphic designer in the neighborhood who will work with residents to create boundary signs to mark the edge of the neighborhood. These should be silk-screened onto steel or aluminum sheet and fastened to existing streetlight or street-sign poles with metal straps. Most municipal governments will refuse permission for this kind of project. So don't ask. Just go ahead and do it, and make sure you get noticed by local media. City hall will look very bad if it tries to remove the signs once they are up.

Hand-painted street banners

Painting street banners attracts lots of local residents, and the final result is also attractive. When people see their own work on a public street they begin to think of the street as theirs. The new sense of ownership means they begin to care for the street. For some it is also the first step to taking on other matters considered to be the business of government.

Signs slow cars, & divert drug dealers

Residents of block-long Rose Street in Vancouver have hand-painted "cat" signs that identify the street and ask motorists to slow down. Signs referring to kids playing also help to warn off street drug dealers, who suspect the neighborhood is full of hostile mothers.

The street as a community blackboard

In another Vancouver project, residents seeking to create a linear park on Jackson Street painted a mural showing their ideas on the street surface. The mural changed the street from a conduit for cars into a forum for public discussion.

A community fence

Two hundred children and adults created 400 highly individual pickets to make a fence for a community garden. Following a practice common to many community art projects, two local artists were hired to train local residents, who drew and then carved their personal statements on the fence. People without any woodworking experience – seniors, parents and children, people with disabilities, and members of many different ethnic groups – became part-time sculptors.

Visioning exercises

Guided visioning exercises have become popular in many fields as a way to define and achieve a desirable future. Studies have shown that athletes are more likely to reach an objective if they can see it and can imagine the steps to reach it. High-jumpers use this technique. They regularly take the time to imagine themselves going through the steps of jumping higher than they have ever jumped before.

Citizens can use visioning to create images that will bring about real improvements to the city. In a typical visioning exercise a facilitator asks participants to close their eyes and imagine they are walking through their neighborhood *as it should be 15 years into the future*. What do they see? What do the buildings look like? Where do people gather? How do they make decisions? What are they eating? Where are they working? How are they traveling? What is happening on the street? Where is the center of the neighborhood? How do green space and water fit into the picture? What do they see when they walk around after dark? People record their visions in diagrams, sketches, models, photographic montages, and written briefs. Sometimes a professional illustrator may help to turn mental images into drawings of the city that people can extend and modify.

Listening projects/Story projects

A New York citizens group wanted to identify what issues would motivate people to become involved in addressing the problems of a low-income neighborhood. They decided to use an informal technique called a listening survey to discover what aroused the most emotional energy.

A group of residents agreed to conduct the survey for a small honorarium. In preparation they held several workshops where they talked about the common blocks to listening, how to eavesdrop in public places, how to get permission to insert yourself into a conversation, how to keep people talking without intruding, and how to deal with people who say something you dislike.

After the exercises they wrote down all the places where different people gathered, plus the names of people whom everyone talked to such as hairdressers and bartenders. Then they formed pairs and went out to the places listed to find people. To conduct the survey, one person encouraged people to talk, while the other acted as recorder. At the end of each week, everyone got together to evaluate the material collected and determine where the strongest feelings lay. Both residents and service providers were surveyed in this way. The results of both surveys were then made available to the whole community.

A close relative of the listening project is the story project. It can focus on gathering the history of an area or capturing the character of an area. Listening and story projects provide good excuses for bringing people together.

4.4   Celebrations

Block parties

Block parties give neighbors a chance to meet one another in a relaxed setting. To hold a successful block party, do some advance planning. A couple of months ahead, start thinking about dates, activities, and supplies. At the same time start enlisting the help of neighbors; find out how they can help and what they can supply. Try to involve as many people as possible, and make sure everyone stays in touch with one another.

Block parties can be held in backyards, neighborhood parks, or on the street. If you close the street, some municipalities may require liability insurance, traffic barricades, and the approval of affected neighbors.

A block party can be any shape or size. It can come at the end of a block cleanup, a block garage sale, or a day of tree-planting. It can have a theme, such as a harvest festival, Canada Day, or Fourth of July celebration. Whatever the nature of your first party, the next will be much easier to organize. On some blocks it becomes an important annual event.

Block yard sales

A block yard sale is easier to organize than a block party. Aim for a Saturday or Sunday afternoon. When the whole block holds a sale you can take advantage of more notices and better signs. More people will also come, drawn by the allure of multiple piles of junk in one location. Block yard sales introduce residents to one another during the planning and during the event.

With so much time spent shopping, many families feel a pressing need to get rid of large quantities of stuff every year in order to have room for new stuff. This has lead to block yard sales becoming annual events on more and more residential blocks. Think of it as a small contribution from material culture that has otherwise undermined local community.

Street reclaiming

Street reclaiming helps people address neighborhood traffic problems and make the street a safer place for families and neighbors to socialize. It can be a spontaneous act done by one person or a neighborhood project that brings a community together.

Street reclaiming changes the psychological feel of a street, making it an "outdoor living room" rather than a thoroughfare overrun by traffic.

Examples of street-reclaiming projects include community-designed "wiggly" streetscapes that slow traffic, celebrations in the street, art on the street, gardens on the street, reading on the sidewalk, and other activities that fill the streets with people.

For more info see Better Environmentally Sound Transportation's *How to Reclaim your Streets: A Community Guidebook,* available on-line at *www.best.bc.ca.* See also *www.playforchange.com.*

Festivals

Most cities and towns have numerous festivals, but most can benefit from having more. A festival can focus on culture such as a Greek or Japanese festival; on religion such as the Vaisakhi (celebrating the birth of Khalsa); or on sport such as a dragon boat festival. It can celebrate some aspect of the performing arts such as a fringe theater festival, a folk festival, or a children's festival. It can also be a contest such as a soap-box derby or kite-flying contest.

In Vancouver, one well-attended community celebration is Illuminares, held on a summer evening around the edge of a small lake. It features stilt walkers, floating pyrotechnics, actors, singers, and a moving procession of light created by hundreds of candle-lit lanterns. During months of preparation, the Public Dreams Society organizes lantern-building workshops for artists, children, and local residents. For Illuminares the community is not only the audience, but also the players, designers, and stagehands.

Parades

Parades are easier to organize and require fewer resources than festivals. Parades usually celebrate a person, a place, an event, or an identity. There are the usual gay pride parades, Canada Day or Fourth of July parades, football parades, and various ethnic parades. But there is no reason why you can't devise your own parade, perhaps to celebrate something that never gets celebrated.

Every July the Public Dreams Society organizes Illuminares in Vancouver. Lead by musicians, people from all over the city proceed around Trout Lake carrying glowing lanterns they have made in workshops leading up to the event. Photo: Tim Matheson.

CHAPTER 5

Practices That Build Community and Democracy

THE COLLECTION OF PRACTICES described in this chapter either build community by maintaining contact between people, or build democracy by increasing civic engagement.

5.1 Practices that Depend on Exchange

Intergenerational activities

Activities that bring young and old together revive a social arrangement that was taken for granted in the past and is still important in many traditional cultures. Bringing old and young together promotes mutual care, transmits cultural values, and enriches the lives of everyone involved.

Some projects bring seniors and children together to focus on a community problem. In one, for instance, high school students and seniors share their experience of alcohol and substance abuse.

In some cities, a Volunteer Grandparents Society matches children aged 3 to 12 who have no grandparent with volunteer grandparents, creating "extended families" that see each other regularly and participate in group events and outings.

An oral history project is another way of bringing seniors and young people together. Typically, young people locate, record, and edit stories and reminiscences of the elderly. They deposit the edited recordings in the public library, where they become an archive of local history.

Child-minding co-ops

If you have small children, you know how difficult it can be to find and pay for a baby-sitter. Child-minding co-ops provide a solution to child-care and a connection to other parents living nearby. In a co-op, parents care for groups of children both in their own homes and in the homes of other parents during the day, evening, or overnight. Most co-ops keep track of baby-sitting hours on a list of debits and credits; one keeps track by exchanging poker chips. Hours are not only determined by the clock, but also by tardiness, the number of children, how late it is when the parents return, and other considerations.

Most co-ops serve a small area, which allows participants to walk between each other's homes. A co-op works best with 15 to 20 families – enough to spread the baby-sitting around. Participants are usually found by talking to friends. This is preferable to posting "vacancies," since most people feel happier leaving their children with "friends of friends."

A selection committee usually visits a candidate's home to look at general safety, neatness, and the level of child-proofing, and to see whether people smoke inside and who might be coming and going. Once they are accepted, candidates pay a small start-up fee and register their names with the co-op's secretary (a position rotated on a monthly or quarterly basis). The secretary is the person who takes "orders" for baby-sitting, usually with a minimum 24 hours' notice. Baby-sitters are sought on the basis of their availability and the balance on their baby-sitting account.

Some co-ops meet every two months for a potluck. It's an occasion to socialize, to introduce new candidates, and to deal with any concerns. Others hold a social event three times a year for both kids and parents. These events bring a sense of community to a sometimes isolated group of parents.

Many co-ops last for as long as 20 years. The longevity of the co-op depends on the ease of administration and the ability to find new families as others outgrow its services.

Walking school-bus

In *Street Reclaiming*, David Engwicht describes an attractive alternative to the practice of parents driving their kids to school. With a walking school-bus, kids walk to school as a group with a parent "driver"; the "bus" scoops up kids along a predetermined route. The walking school-bus increases contact between kids living in a neighborhood and between parent volunteers. It also reduces traffic and gives everyone a little exercise.

Community kitchens

Community kitchens provide an opportunity for people to get together to share the cost, planning, and preparation of healthy meals. Members usually meet twice a month: once to plan four or five entrees and to organize the purchase of food, and once to prepare the meals. Since a licensed kitchen is not required, groups meet in homes as well as church basements, neighborhood houses, and community centers.

Specialty kitchens are common. In Vancouver, one "cultural kitchen" provides an opportunity for Vietnamese women to learn about Canadian food products and how they are prepared. Another has a "canning kitchen" where participants put up canned goods such as fruit, tomatoes, and jam. Other kitchens specialize in vegetarian, ethnic, and special needs cooking. The interests of the group decide the focus of the kitchen.

Community kitchens are popular for a variety of reasons. Food costs less because it can be bought in bulk. It also takes less time to prepare because it is cooked in quantity – and sometimes frozen for later use. Apart from the food, people appreciate the way community kitchens provide an excuse for people to get together. Many people have become close friends through community cooking. Some have discovered common interests that have led to the formation of new groups focusing on a variety of social issues. To find out about local community kitchens contact your local community center or community health clinic.

River guardians

River guardians look after a river by regularly walking a stretch of riverbank. Sometimes they do water tests, sometimes they report suspicious discharges to authorities. Different people looking out for different stretches of water can keep an eye on a river hundreds of miles long – something that would be impossibly expensive for government to do alone. A stewardship society usually trains volunteers and tries to make sure it has all the critical stretches covered.

Guarding rivers has many spin-off benefits. When seniors participate they feel they can still make a worthwhile contribution to society. For others the project becomes a daily walk and a way of getting exercise. If two people or two families do the job, it helps to build community by establishing a regular pattern of contact. For more information on river guarding, check out the website of the Willamette Riverkeepers in Oregon.

Sharing networks

Sharing networks bring people together and prevent pointless consumption. There is no reason why all the people on a city block need their own lawnmower, their own 20-foot ladder, or their own hedge trimmer. All of these things can be shared. Problems of availability, maintenance, and repair are easy to address. Availability is not an issue for seldom-used items. Maintenance and repair are manageable if everyone pays a small annual fee. Member-managed sharing networks work best when they are small (two to six neighbors) and when members enjoy one another's company.

Sharing resources helps to promote spontaneous encounters. Introducing new technology, by reducing the need to share, often seems to have the opposite effect. In many Third World villages, women would meet at the village well, a shared resource. When water was piped into houses, accidental encounters at the well disappeared and so did a large chunk of village social life. In British households, everyone used to congregate in the kitchen, where it was warm. With the introduction of central heating, family members retreated to separate rooms, reducing the social interaction in the household. In large cities, people who commute by car are cut off from others when they travel to and from work. Other technologies seem to have a similar effect. Studies of the social impact of the telephone, sewing machine, television, personal computer, further illustrate the bias of technology for privacy.

Sharing systems can help to counteract the drift into private worlds. Vanpools and carpools, for instance, can recreate social connections that were destroyed by the introduction of the personal automobile.

Pro bono networks

In large cities people have more services – if they can pay. A pro bono network provides services for people who can't pay and for worthwhile projects that are short of funds.

The first step in creating a pro bono network is to find out who is willing to help, then to ask how much and in what way each person can help. Most designers, engineers, scientists, doctors, printers, accountants, teachers, and other professional, service, and trades people are willing to contribute a little time to community and other public interest work. Lawyers in particular have stepped forward to create pro bono networks that provide legal assistance to poor people and non-profit organizations.

A good network requires a good coordinator who can make it easy for people to contribute. The coordinator's main job is to match requests for help with those who have indicated a willingness to help. A coordinator may also develop ways to address problems associated with clients undervaluing what they do not pay for. Of some help in preventing undervaluing are clear written agreements, actual bills with waivers, and tax receipts for services contributed

Reciprocal care

Because our culture commodifies everything, people have increasingly come to obtain social goods from paid professionals rather than friends, neighbors, and relatives. The elderly for instance often rely on health care professionals for someone to talk to. But the elderly can rely on one another. They can find company in seniors centers, and two people can check up on one another by telephoning or visiting every day.

Reciprocal caring can also work for people with different needs. Consider the success of combining an old folks home and a day-care facility. It revives a practice common in traditional communities where the elderly looked after children. In the past, caring for kids gave the elderly a sense of purpose, and it freed adults to do other work. Today, most seniors say they don't find the idea at all attractive, but create an actual opportunity for old people and kids to interact and watch what happens.

Reciprocal care can take other forms, some quite small. A person might feed a cat or water plants while neighbors are away on vacation. They might return the favor. These kinds of exchanges build community and solve practical problems at the same time.

Care doesn't even have to be reciprocal to benefit the care-giver. An Institute for the Advancement of Health study of 1700 women who regularly volunteered to help others produced a surprising result. Over fifty percent reported a "helpers high", a mild euphoria that returned when ever they recalled their volunteer work. They also felt more energetic, less depressed; and experienced an increased sense of self worth. Paradoxically, the best way to "look out for number-one" might be to look out for others.

5.2   Practices that Promote Democracy

Awards for contributions to local democracy

Giving awards for small steps in the right direction is one of the least expensive and most pleasant ways of building democracy. Awards for contributions to local democracy can be given out to government workers (usually municipal bureaucrats) who go beyond the call of duty to involve citizens.

In Vancouver, a citizens group put out a public call for nominations, then a small committee reviewed written material supporting each nomination. Because the committee decided it would be smart not to limit the number of winners, every nominee received a very large framed award designed by a local graphic designer. Winners were astonished. No one had ever recognized the work of bureaucrats before. Most awards ended up on office walls. Some went up in the lobby areas of city hall, where they continue to remind everyone of what really matters.

Good neighbor awards

To identify people for good neighbor awards, put nomination boxes around the neighborhood in coffee shops, libraries, schools, and community centers. The nomination box should bear the name of the project and a few lines of instructions. Nominations should include the name and address of the person nominated, why they are being nominated, and the name and address of the person making the nomination.

It's important that every legitimate nominee get an award. Some well-meaning organizations, focusing on outstanding service, choose to recognize only a few people. This is a mistake. By giving out lots of awards you encourage lots of people to think of themselves as good neighbors. This has an upward spiraling effect, encouraging more neighborliness and more small acts that create attractive social places.

Present the awards at a brief ceremony in a public place. Issue a media advisory before the event and a press release after.

Citizens juries

A citizens jury is a forum where citizens can address a complex or contentious issue. Juries are usually organized by a neutral nonprofit organization devoted to democracy building. The project begins by hiring a polling company to identify a large random pool of potential jurors. This pool is boiled down to a representative group of jurors who are ideally a microcosm of the community from which they are drawn.

The jury receives a charge – one or more questions it must try to answer – and is briefed on the issue. Jurors then hear evidence over three or four days from experts and various intervenors. They ask questions, discuss the issue among themselves, and finally issue a "verdict."

The project organizer must take care to ensure all sides of an issue are represented and that biases do not creep in during the selection of jurors, the presentation of information, or the choice of witnesses.

Jury "verdicts" are usually recommendations for how government or some other public body should act. Because of this the project organizer usually tries to get some prior commitment from the public body to take the recommendations seriously and provide a genuine response.

Citizens juries get good reviews when they are properly organized. They build citizen capacity and reduce public suspicion when decisions are eventually made in line with jury recommendations. Some political scientists have suggested that citizens juries should review every proposed new law as a way of democratizing government. On the downside, citizen juries are expensive and tend to involve relatively small numbers of citizens.

To avoid accusations of bias, a jury needs to be run by an organization with a reputation for complete neutrality. Little-known organizations need to assemble a public oversight committee that includes respected people such as retired judges, church ministers, and even-handed journalists.

In England, the Local Government Management Board has experience running citizens juries. In the US, the Jefferson Center has developed a successful citizens jury process.

Rating candidates for public office

Since 1911 the Municipal League of Kings County (Seattle) has been assembling evaluation committees that rate candidates seeking public office. Seattle papers publish the recommendations of these committees as a guide for voters who do not have the time to investigate candidates in depth.

The Municipal League begins by assembling an unbiased committee that will evaluate political candidates as if they were people applying for a job. The League tries to ensure the committee is a microcosm of the voting community, with members representing a mix of age, sex, education, income, ethnic background, and political orientation. The League asks various organizations to participate, then asks individuals who come forward to fill out a questionnaire. One of the questions asks would-be evaluators to define their place on the political spectrum by putting an x on a scale that ranges from far right to far left. Using this and other information, a group of former evaluation committee members select a balanced range of people for the new committee.

The new committee receives some training before it goes to work. It then reviews background material on the candidates, including press clippings and the candidates' resumes. The committee also checks the references supplied by the candidates. Next, the committee interviews each candidate for half an hour with a predetermined set of revealing questions.

Following the interview, committee members score candidates for
- *knowledge* (candidates should be well-versed in major issues),
- *involvement* (candidates should have a record of community service and be familiar with their constituents),
- *character* (candidates should be free of questionable character attributes and questionable history), and
- *effectiveness* (incumbents should have a proven record of accomplishments in office; challengers should be able to demonstrate success in past endeavors).

A candidate evaluation project is a good way to sidestep the influence of money and elect better people to public office, but it requires resources and a credible organization to sponsor the project. Little-known organizations will need a media partner and respected people to oversee the process.

5.3   Practices that Promote Community

Promoting spontaneous encounters

Modern cities have greatly reduced the opportunities for spontaneous or accidental encounters. Spontaneous encounters have advantages over planned encounters for several reasons. They are more frequent. (How many times have you intended to get together with a friend and never got around to it?) They are also less demanding, less time-consuming, and more varied. In the past, most accidental encounters occurred on the street.

Over time, without anyone much noticing, the street became less and less a place for spontaneous meeting. Increasing automobile traffic drove people away, at the same separating people living on opposite sides of the street.

The loss of the street as the main site for social encounters severely damaged cities. Besides being places for commercial exchange, cities are places for the exchange of culture, services, friendship, and inspiration. According to David Engwicht in *Reclaiming our Cities and Towns,* we can bring some of this back if we begin to see streets as destinations, instead of ways to get to destinations.

We can also design physical space to promote rather than discourage spontaneous encounters. The so-called new urbanism tries to promote spontaneous encounters by reintroducing elements of the small town. Houses with verandas placed close to the sidewalk encourage exchanges with passersby. Cars parked on the street encourage the chance meeting of neighbors as they come and go.

Converted houses that have shared bathrooms, shared laundry, and other shared facilities promote encounters between residents. Co-housing promotes accidental encounters by introducing interior streets, shared meals, and shared special-use rooms. Congregate housing for the elderly promotes accidental encounters by combining tiny private units with a large common dining room and common areas dedicated to other special uses.

Coffee rooms, photocopy rooms, mailbox areas, and other shared facilities can be sites for spontaneous encounters. As such, they encourage informal feedback, allow efficient ad hoc work, and improve the relationships between workers in different parts of the same organization. Because certain types of creative work thrive on unplanned social interaction, some organizations provide "project space" in the form of white boards in shared areas.

Crosstalk cafés

In the past, salons and café culture were crucibles for social change. A crosstalk café is an attempt to reawaken café culture by encouraging patrons to talk to people they don't know or don't know well.

A crosstalk cafe is not a hangout. People go to a hangout hoping to meet people they already know. But crosstalk cafés and hangouts are both places to connect with others spontaneously.

In a typical coffee joint, most people sit by themselves. Conversations between strangers are short and isolated. Conversations in a crosstalk café are longer, overlapping, and include many people. They occur between tables, crisscrossing the café space.

Because of the bias for privacy and isolation created by consumer society, crosstalk cafés don't occur naturally; they need to be consciously created. In particular, they require practices that bring people together, such as waiters taking the time to introduce people to one another. At a real crosstalk café, the quality of social interaction is as important as the quality of the coffee.

Salons

Salons are small groups of people who gather together primarily for conversation. Since their origins in the Enlightenment of the 18th and in 19th century France, salons have been associated with social change. They bring to mind Margaret Mead's often-quoted observation: "Never doubt that a small group of thoughtful, committed citizens can change the world: indeed it's the only thing that ever has." Jurgen Habermas, in *The Structural Transformation of the Public Sphere,* attributes even more importance to salons, connecting them to café culture and the birth of the public sphere.

In the past, well-connected aristocratic women would organize a salon. The salonieres' first job was to compose the salon for the best result. They would decide who to invite to ensure a mix of the brightest and wittiest people. The right mix of people and perspectives was and still is necessary for a lively conversation.

A small number of people works best for salons, just as it does for other forms of community. Limit the size to ten people or less if you want everyone to be part of the same discussion. Invite people with different backgrounds who will enjoy one another's company.

Unofficial salon etiquette

- No leaders
- Allow and address the silence
- No dialogue
- No cross-talk
- No advice giving, just "I" statements

In a seminal 1991 *Utne Reader* article, Stephanie Mills presented an unofficial etiquette for salons. Mills admits the result of this etiquette isn't exactly conversation. It may be closer to people making little speeches. So you might try your own variations and include real dialogue. *Utne Reader* and New Society have since published *Salons: The Joy of Conversation*, a guide to setting up and running a salon.

Closely related to salons are kitchen-table discussion groups, reading circles and study circles.

Kitchen-table discussion groups

A kitchen-table discussion group is a small group of people, often neighbors, who get together in someone's home to talk, listen, and share ideas on subjects of mutual interest. The host encourages people to listen, to ask clarifying questions, and to avoid arguing or interrupting. The host points out that there are no right or wrong ideas and generally tries to foster engaging conversation.

Reading circles

Reading circles resemble college seminar groups except they are organized by participants. The circle agrees on a book worth reading, which everyone reads, then gets together to discuss. If the task of reading is difficult, the group might break the book into chunks, then meet to discuss each chunk. For a more interesting discussion, half of the group might read one book while the other half reads a contrasting book. Another variation is to have different people present different books. This way, participants can learn about 8 to 10 books for every one they have to read. Where a book is particularly important, two people might present on the same book, or each person could present a different part of the same book.

Study circles

A study circle is a group of 8 to 12 people who meet regularly to hear a presentation from a member of the group or an invited outsider. There are so many variations of the study circle that it would be misleading to describe one or two variations as the best. Typically, most form around a common interest that determines their focus. Many order in food or combine study sessions with dinner to foster a healthy social atmosphere. Some go beyond reading and discussion, and consider possibilities for creative action.

Community-wide study circles

Sometimes local government or a community foundation will organize a large number of study circles to deal with a difficult community problem or public policy issue. A community-wide study circles project requires funding for promotion, a paid organizer, and paid facilitators. Each circle meets for two-hour sessions at least three times. The US Study Circles Resource Center provides an on-line facilitation training manual and a step-by-step guide for getting a community-wide study circles project underway.

Community-wide study circles provide an opportunity for public education and public deliberation, and help to bridge the gap between public policy and public attitudes. Participants spend time on what Daniel Yankelovich, in *Coming to Public Judgment,* calls "working through," where they examine the consequences of taking different stands on an issue in order to come to a relatively stable point of view.

New community partnerships

John Kretzmann and John McKnight, in their book *Building Communities from the Inside Out,* show how we can bring communities back to life if we focus on local assets rather than on local needs. By beginning a community development process with a needs assessment, community workers unwittingly lead people to see themselves as needy and dependent. When looking at low-income neighborhoods, the authors say, we have to stop seeing the glass as half empty and begin to see it as half full. We need to identify, then build on, strengths latent in the community.

The way to start building a community is to identify its resources: local individuals, institutions, and associations. This process usually turns up far more active groups and individuals in an area than anyone ever imagined. In one 24-block neighborhood in Chicago, researchers found 230 associations of various kinds – artistic, business, charitable, church, collectors, elderly, ethnic, health, hobby, men's, self-help, neighborhood, outdoors, political, school, service, social cause, sports, study, veterans, women's, and youth.

Kretzmann and McKnight provide hundreds of examples of what happens when normally separate fragments of a community begin working in partnership with one another. They show how local seniors, disabled persons, welfare recipients, and artists can work with schools, parks, libraries, community colleges, police, and hospitals to produce truly impressive results.

All sorts of other activities

The preceding list of community building activities only hints at the opportunities for meeting people and building community at the local level. Other possibilities are limited only by your imagination. They might include joining or creating groups like the following:

- A garden club that exchanges cuttings and advice
- A parks committee
- A car cooperative that provides inexpensive access to a car
- A broad network that gets together at the same time every week at a community café or local hangout
- A group that creates and manages a local currency system
- A community mapping group
- A Toastmaster's club
- A neighborhood brewing circle to batch brew beer
- A local baseball, soccer, volleyball, hockey, boccie ball team
- A seniors club that arranges excursions
- A local historical society that unearths local history
- A diner's club that eats its way around local restaurants
- A kids sports group
- A local jogging, exercise, or tai-chi club
- A local food co-op that provides inexpensive food in exchange for a small contribution of time
- A group that volunteers after-hour services to those in need
- A local theatre group
- A local singing group
- A local design panel that comments on proposed development
- A local earthquake preparedness group
- A local welcoming committee for new residents

Dinos Against Fossil Fuels ride around on bicycles, singing bad songs, and waving Extinction Stinks signs to protest car culture. Each dino wears a suit made from cloth, coroplast, and inner tube for a tail hinge.

CHAPTER **6**

Preventing Grassroots Wilt

M UCH OF THE LITERATURE on citizen participation is too optimistic. The enthusiasm for what might be accomplished
with more active citizens seems to blind those who write about
the subject. An overly optimistic outlook encourages people to
step out of private life, but sets them up to become quickly dis-
couraged. This chapter looks at the forces that undermine
grassroots groups and active citizens and suggests practical ways
to overcome these sources of "grassroots wilt."

6.1   GRASSROOTS WILT 1 Lack of Time

In 1999 the US League of Women Voters (LWV) commissioned a
study titled *Working Together: Community Involvement in
America,* which consisted of one-to-one interviews with activists,
group interviews with citizens in four cities, and a national survey. According to the LWV study, the main barrier to citizen
participation is lack of time. See Appendix 4 "How to Increase
Community Participation". The study showed that many people
viewed community involvement as direct competition for time
spent with family and friends. Nevertheless, 46 percent of
Americans say they would like to be more involved in their communities.

Provide more scheduling alternatives. The long-term solution
to the problem of lack of time is to convince people to reduce
consumption so they can reduce the amount of time spent working and increase their discretionary free time. The short-term
solution is to figure out new ways of fitting community contributions into hectic lives. The study offers some practical suggestions:

- Make it possible for volunteers to work flexible hours and short one- to two-hour periods.
- Make it possible for people to decide what work they will do and how they will do it.
- Make it possible for volunteers to get out of a commitment on an ad hoc basis.
- Make it possible for volunteers to contribute with children, family, and friends.

Emphasize the value of each person's contribution. The study points out that, "given their busy schedules, people want reassurance that their work will make a difference and that their time will not be wasted. Organizers should explain how a volunteer's work will benefit others and the community. They should also explain the importance of the problem being addressed.

"The two strongest messages out of the survey include one message that urges people to take ownership of their communities, get involved and make a difference, and another message that talks about joining together to make a practical, tangible difference in the lives of those that are most important – our families, children, friends and neighbors."

Organize around children. In the LWV survey the highest number (a quarter of respondents) said the helping, mentoring, and coaching of children and youth would be the most likely incentive to make them become involved in their community.

Provide information about your group and its activities. The second most important issue affecting involvement is whether or not a project is worthy of involvement. People want to know whether the project and the people behind it are legitimate and competent. Disengaged participants want an honest and "fearless" leader with organizational and planning skills, enthusiasm, and a good attitude.

6.2   GRASSROOTS WILT 2   Self-destructive Group Behavior

One largely overlooked cause of low levels of citizen involvement is the internal dynamics of all-volunteer groups. Countless grassroots initiatives wither and die without achieving anything because members don't pay attention to what can go wrong inside a group. Many citizens groups quite simply drive away their most able members. In a typical arc, a new member will step forward to work with others on some public issue, last for a relatively short time, then disappear back into private life, never to be heard from again. A flash of green, then nothing. What causes this kind of wilt?

Too little fun. People who take themselves too seriously can turn any task into a chore. Getting together should feel more like recreation than work, no matter how serious the issue. Long-term activists have fun when they get together. They almost always enjoy making fun of people in power. Those who understand citizen involvement stress the importance of having fun over all other considerations.

Too much emphasis on organization and too little on mission. Hoping to become more organized, many small groups create little bureaucracies that drain everyone's energy. Often so much effort goes into maintaining the organization that there is little left to pursue the reason for creating an organization in the first place. Beware of creating a board, forming a non-profit society, writing grant applications, fundraising, annual reports, *Robert's Rules of Order,* and the other components of organizational quicksand.

Too many meetings and too little action. Most people would prefer to act on something concrete rather than sit at a meeting wrangling over an issue trying to "reach consensus." Some meetings are necessary, but try to keep the frequency down, the length short, and the number of participants small.

Too much deciding and too little creating. Every advocacy group needs to generate options for action. To do this well, participants need to switch off their Voice of Judgment and brainstorm. Unfortunately, when people get together for a meeting they usually switch on their Voice of Judgment in preparation for decision making. If they remain in this critical frame of mind, they will generate few options for action, little will get done, and no one will have any fun.

Too many people. Because of the emphasis on getting more people involved, many people feel that large groups are better than small groups. This is a mistake. A working group should not exceed ten people. A small group does not preclude working with others under the umbrella of a larger group; nor does it prelude communicating with larger numbers of people through e-mail networks, special events, and annual conventions.

Too little contact. It is hard for people to maintain a working relationship if they rarely see one another. Once a month is the usual minimum for long-term projects. Once a week is best for hot or short-term projects. Once a week also fits the way people schedule other activities. If regular face-to-face contact is difficult, regular phone calls or e-mail may work as a weak substitute. Community groups need to pay more attention to unplanned contact. Much of it used to occur on the street. Today it occurs in the workplace, in places designed to enhance community such as co-housing, and, in Great Britain, in pubs.

Too much to do. Groups of nine or less can often manage on personal resources, but as group size increases and there is more to do, a shortage of money and time often leads to spiraling decline. Without paid staff there is no one to look after organizational housekeeping, and no one to train, manage, and reward volunteers. As people disappear, many grassroots leaders burn out trying to do more and more themselves. A lack of resources does not mean giving up. It means keeping your group small, and inventing clever ways to use time, connections, and skills. Most important it means matching what you do to the resources you have available.

For more on dealing with destructive group behavior see Chapters 1 and 2, in particular 1.9 "Keeping People Involved."

6.3 GRASSROOTS WILT 3 Tiny Fiefdoms

A recent Canadian sociology textbook dismissed grassroots citizens groups as irrelevant sociologically and politically because they were small and fragmented.

It's the *combination* of small and fragmented that is the problem. By itself, "small" is an asset, but small groups only become significant players when they cooperate with other groups. When they all do their own thing and ignore, or avoid cooperating with others, they have a hard time addressing anything beyond small local issues.

Most activists know that fragmentation inhibits effective action. Nevertheless activist groups that could benefit from cooperating with one another frequently ignore or criticize one another. Neighborhood groups operating in the same part of town often squabble among themselves. Non-profits working on the same issue often denigrate one another. Some of this is understandable.

GROWTH STAGES OF GRASSROOTS GROUPS

Psychologists Bruce Tuckman and Mary Jensen have shown that groups evolve through five stages.

Forming. During this get-acquainted stage the team tries to define its collective goals and figure out how to reach them with the skills and abilities each member brings to the table.

Storming. Chaos takes over as opinions and conflicts begin to surface. Members may argue about priorities and responsibilities. Some may drop out because of the tension and disagreements that develop. This is the most difficult stage for any group, but one that is manageable if people are prepared for it.

Norming. Members begin to bond with each other and the team acquires an identity. There's a sense of unity and a "can-do" attitude.

Performing. At this stage, which is the most difficult to reach, the group becomes a smoothly running team firing on all cylinders. Interaction and communication become second nature. Members decide by consensus. Conflicts are rare.

Adjourning. Although some groups may continue indefinitely, some task-oriented groups may disband when they have achieved their goals.

Many groups are uncooperative because they compete with other groups for funds, official status, or media attention.

Many also have an inward focus and an us-versus-them orientation that promotes suspicion of outsiders and a desire to operate independently.

Hostility to outsiders may also come from a leader who wants full control over a "tiny fiefdom." Beyond the group, at home or at work, this person might have very little authority. For a fish that is big because the pond is small, cooperation and coalition building look like a threat, a recipe for undermining one's authority should smarter or more aggressive people appear on the scene.

Tiny fiefdoms wilt fast

Failure to cooperate with other groups leads to rapid wilt because it severely limits what a group can accomplish. People drop out when they see the group is going nowhere. Eventually the group withers to a de facto leader and a small collection of followers with limited expectations.

Incandescent citizens are not the answer

At the centers of many tiny fiefdoms are incandescent citizens, dedicated people who work relentlessly on projects they have taken on. Often they accomplish a great deal and get a lot of media attention. But their heroic efforts do little to build civil society. They undermine broader citizen involvement by grabbing the limelight and by sidelining those who can't match their commitment or know-how. Eventually most of them burn out, leaving a hole that is hard to fill.

The best way to prevent this kind of wilt is to make sure that more than one person shares in leading the group, and to make sure cooperation with outsiders is part of the group's culture.

6.4   GRASSROOTS WILT 4   Corrosive People

If there is one phrase heard more than any other in community development it's "Be inclusive." Most people accept this as good and necessary. After all, most communities are diverse, and community building involves working with others. But the literature on community development ignores a major problem. Being inclusive can lead to the rapid decline and destruction of a citizens group.

There is no problem if being inclusive means including people of different races, different religions, different ethnicity, different sex or sexual orientation. And there is no problem if being inclusive means including people who hold different views. Problems arise when being inclusive means including people who prevent the group from functioning in a reasonably healthy manner. Few are willing to admit what is obvious in any grassroots group: some people are assets and others are liabilities. Occasionally a single person will be sufficiently corrosive to destroy the whole group.

An effective chair can often manage one or two corrosive people. But even the best chair will have trouble with people who drive everyone nuts, people who are very angry or very combative or very controlling or very long-winded or really out-to-lunch. One or two constantly disruptive or offensive people can wear everyone down.

The worst part is that good people begin to leave. They ask themselves, "Why should I spend my free time putting up with this?" And they vanish. As more good people leave, the influence of a corrosive person increases, causing more good people to leave. The downhill spiral usually continues until the group is reduced to a grim residue of hard-core meeting attenders and marginal people desperate for any kind of human contact.

Corrosion prevention

So how does one prevent this kind of decline? First, avoid opening the door to all comers when creating a core group or steering committee. See 1.3 "Forming a Core Group". Don't ask for volunteers for important committees; identify people who will work well together and invite them to take part. If you wish to open the door to everyone, do it at a large annual event, where the impact of disruptive people will be diluted by other people. If a corrosive person penetrates your group, you may be forced to remedy the situation by arranging meetings through selective invitation. Another way is to ask for a volunteer willing to meet separately with the corrosive person. The volunteer would brush up on conflict resolution, then gently ask the person to leave the group.

Lack of congeniality on a larger scale

Z Magazine founder Michael Albert considers a broader version of the corrosion problem in *The Trajectory of Change.* He starts by wondering how many people have been involved in progressive change in the last 30 years. How many people have been involved in the civil rights movement, various anti-war movements, the no-nukes movement, the women's movement, left electoral campaigns, student movements, green movements, and community actions? How many have taken a course from a radical teacher, gone to a progressive talk, or taken part in a gay or lesbian action, a pro-choice campaign, union organizing, an anti-racist project, a demonstration, march, strike, or boycott? Ten million is a conservative estimate, Albert concludes. Then he asks, "Of these millions of people, how many are still active members of Team Change?" Very few. Over the long term we need to hold on to people once we have attracted them. If large numbers of people pull out, we'll always be short of the numbers needed for large-scale progressive change.

So why do people leave? Let's look, says Albert, at someone who becomes more and more involved in progressive work.

> *Does this person merge into a growing community of people, feel more secure and appreciated, feel a growing sense of personal worth and of contribution to something valuable, and enjoy a sense of accomplishment? . . Or does this person meet a lot of other people who continually question her motives and behavior, making her feel insecure and constantly criticized? Does this person feel diminishing personal worth and doubt that what he or she is doing is making a difference? . . Does she have needs that were previously met but are now unmet? . . Is this person's life getting more frustrating, less enjoyable?*

All too often this is just what happens. So good people simply leave. They discover progressive culture is unappealing and uncongenial. They discover it's more about whining than winning. And they discover, in its obsession with taking care of the world, it fails to take care of the very people it needs to get the job done. See also "Grassroots Wilt 9: Leaving everyone behind."

6.5 GRASSROOTS WILT 5 Activist Motivations

Some motivations lead to wilt; others are essential for success.

Propelled by a desire to change the world

All activists want to change the world or some little corner of it. Moreover, most activists think they can actually pull it off. This more than anything else distinguishes activists from bystanders. The view that nothing will ever change, that citizen action is hopeless, and that opposition is too powerful discourages people from becoming active. For this reason most books that try to encourage people to become active devote a lot of space to stories that show ordinary people with limited resources can in fact change the world.

Propelled by anger

Anger, especially "hot anger", presents many problems as a prime motivator. First, people are mistrustful of those who are always angry. Second, no one wants to be around people who are always angry. Third, anger works against group process, making it hard to have fun, plan strategically, and think creatively.

Finally, when hot anger eventually subsides people tend to retreat back into private life.

Still, many activists would agree that anger provides the energy that motivates them. In searching out community leaders, the Industrial Areas Foundation specifically looks for people with "cold anger" – controlled anger at the injustice they have suffered. For more on the IAF see Appendix 1.

Propelled by heroism

The press often represents public interest activists as saints and heroes. This characterization does nothing to promote the involvement of ordinary citizens because it makes activism seem like the peculiar pursuit of abnormally dedicated people. The hero drives other people away, sometimes out of a desire to control everything, sometimes out of a need to take credit for every success. Whatever the dynamic, the hero usually winds up doing more work as more people drop out, eventually quitting from sheer exhaustion. Heros are similar to the "incandescent citizens" mentioned in Grassroots Wilt 3.

Propelled by empathy

Empathy is a good motivator. Research shows that modest helping contributes to the health of the helper. Paradoxically, looking out for others seems to be the best way to look out for number one. People also enjoy working with those they see as compassionate. People who are empathetic contribute to group process: they listen and they try to see issues from the other person's point of view.

The main problem with empathy by itself is that it is insufficient for situations where confrontation offers the only way forward. Empathetic people can often be bought off with an empty promise, a worthless appointment, or an invitation to a stakeholders meeting.

Propelled by self-interest

Self-interest needs to be present in some form because people are only occasionally altruists. Whether the particular self-interest of an activist is helpful depends on the details. Grassroots efforts flourish when people participate because of social or psychological benefits that come from meeting new people, learning new skills, developing self-confidence, and wielding power through collective action.

Grassroots efforts also flourish when they focus on the interests of a large group of people. They wither when they focus on the narrow self-interest of an individual or a small group of people.

The narrow self-interest of an individual can, however, blossom into something that benefits others. People may become activists accidentally by trying unsuccessfully to resolve a problem that affects themselves or their family. A mother concerned that her son is learning too little in school, for instance, may end up creating a pressure group of concerned parents to advocate for changes to educational practices for a whole city, state, or province.

Propelled by a way of being

Civil society would be in much better shape if large numbers of people viewed public involvement as a normal part of everyday life. Some people do hold this view; often they are people whose parents or friends are involved in regular volunteer work. But their numbers are small.

Most people have adopted the view promoted by governments, corporations, and the corporate mass media that regular public involvement is anything but normal. It's the domain of "special interest groups," whiners, radicals, and troublemakers.

As mentioned earlier, people usually become involved because they have been asked by friends or family. In such cases, the motives for becoming involved may be entirely a matter of interpersonal relationships and have nothing to do with an activist agenda. However, as a result of taking part, new recruits may adopt increasingly more activist views. Thus, motives that encourage activism may follow from involvement as much as lead to it.

Propelled by a sense of personal responsibility

Another healthy motivation comes from the attitude that one must do something, given what is going on. A sense of personal responsibility is the only motivation that can sustain activism in the bleakest times, when little is being accomplished. Amongst activists working for nuclear disarmament, for example, pessimism is often high, but they continue on nevertheless because they feel a moral obligation to do so and because they wish to convince others that they too are morally bound to do so.

In *Watchdogs and Gadflies: Activism from marginal to mainstream*, Tim Falconer quotes Wendy Cukier of the Coalition for Gun Control in Canada on her sense of personal responsibility:

The only thing that makes me different from a lot of other people – aside from a large ego and thinking I can do things, and it not occurring to me that I can't – is a sense of personal responsibility. I grew up with a sense that if you don't stand up for what you believe in, in a very active way, you're a collaborator. I realize when I talk to other people that they think exactly what I think; they read the newspaper and they cry, they're horrified by things that go on, but somehow there's a disconnect between them and all that stuff.

For many potential activists the "disconnect" comes from being overwhelmed – from sensing that so much needs to be done. Those who become involved anyway do so knowing that they cannot do everything, but they can do something meaningful.

6.6   GRASSROOTS WILT 6

Little Citizen-Government Cooperation

Old-fashioned bureaucracies with unresponsive politicians can easily marginalize citizens. Progressive governments can do just the opposite. One only has to visit a progressive city to recognize the enormous impact of a good working relationship between government and citizens. Too many municipal governments and bureaucrats see government's role as service delivery and see citizens as customers or supplicants instead of partners.

What can be done? Below are suggestions for both local government and citizens groups.

Activists need to learn how to work with government

According to John Gardner, founder of the US group Common Cause, "A weakness of citizen action is a disinclination to get a professional grasp of the processes of government. Well-meaning citizens can't be bothered with the grimy machinery by which the public business gets done." A survey of progressive groups would show that those who actually get results do so by working with government.

While many activists limit their work to media advocacy (Chapter 9), evidence shows that media advocacy that targets government is far more effective when coupled with discussions with government. Gar Mahood of the Non-Smokers Rights Association in Canada has succeeded in achieving legislation aimed at reducing the damage caused by smoking despite a well-funded tobacco lobby. "Politicians and bureaucrats take us seriously," he tells Tim Falconer in *Watchdogs and Gadflies*. "To get the ear of government, first you have to show that your advice is worth listening to. Secondly, you have to be able to demonstrate that you can develop public support, that you speak for a substantial body of public opinion. Thirdly, you have to show them that you can punch them in the nose if they don't pay attention."

Public citizens should tackle private citizens

Active citizens, particularly regular members of neighborhood associations, are the right people to address citizen opposition to public interest land use projects such as low-income housing, special needs facilities, and sprawl-reducing multiple housing. The strategies for reducing NIMBY opposition often fail when advanced by people seen as self-serving developers; land use consultants who stand to gain financially; social service workers who seem inclined to place the welfare of their constituents first; and planners who appear to be the pawns of politicians.

Activists should pause before opposing

The impact of development projects can be neutral, positive, or negative. In the absence of hard information, many citizens quickly conclude a project will have a large negative impact. Before drawing conclusions, active citizens should assess a project on objective grounds, and include an assessment of similar projects in other places. Public or foundation money should be available so that public interest groups can undertake this work, especially in areas where there is little trust in government information. Governments need to devise better ways of providing citizens with information they will trust. Activists, on the other hand, need to recognize that knee-jerk citizen opposition undermines the larger project of improving citizen involvement.

Governments should respond when citizens can do more with less

For certain kinds of projects, citizens with adequate resources can do a better job for less money than either contractors or public servants. Citizen volunteers are the only viable alternative in some cases, including: community crime prevention, protecting and restoring rivers, protecting heritage buildings, running large festivals, and looking out for the elderly who are still living at home.

Neighborhood associations can resolve many local problems on their own. Where neighborhood associations have a good working relationship with city government, people take problems to their neighborhood association first. Jeffrey Berry, Kent Portney, and Ken Thomson, the authors of *The Rebirth of Urban Democracy,* found that many problems are resolved here and do not proceed to local government.

Moreover, citizens who understand how cities work inform and moderate the views of those who do not. Citizen-to-citizen interactions tend to be free of suspicion and less likely to slide into abusive behavior. Those who may yell at paid bureaucrats or professional politicians feel they have less right to yell at their neighbors.

Governments should do more to encourage citizen involvement

Governments believe only they have the objectivity and expertise to act in the public interest. Many local governments believe citizens come forth solely for selfish reasons, and they point to numerous examples of NIMBY (Not In My Back Yard) outrage at any new land use proposal. Indeed, some bad behavior is motivated by purely selfish concerns, but often it comes from nothing more than lack of knowledge and lack of trust. Protesting citizens and besieged officials waste a great deal of time and energy on phantom problems created by lack of trust in government, lack of understanding about how cities work, lack of understanding of the constraints on bureaucrats, and lack of understanding of the likely consequences of proposed changes.

Most of these problems are the result of citizens being left out. Government officials often balk at the thought of greater citizen participation because they are so used to facing angry people. They need to hear stories of successful citizen involvement, which will show them that involved, educated people are better behaved.

Governments should require social approval before regulatory approval

Active citizens working at the local level should advocate changes to the way local government deals with development proposals. The usual method requires that developers first get the approval of government and then, after the project has been worked out in detail, the approval of local residents. Progressive cities turn this around. They require developers to approach area residents first. This process takes longer, but it replaces the usual land use conflict with negotiation, and reduces the chance that developers will invest a great deal of money in a project that ends up being halted by opposition at the last moment. This process also eliminates a practice that makes citizens feel they are being consulted after decisions have already been made, which undermines the trust between citizens and government.

Consider the national appetite for government control

In Canada, many community development meetings are short on citizens but chock full of people from government, agencies, non-profits, and institutions funded directly or indirectly by government. The majority of Canadians seem content to allow technocrats to make public decisions that affect every aspect of their lives. The flip side to Canadians' willingness to trust everything to government is government's unwillingness to trust anything to citizens. Thus bureaucrats in Canada treat citizen involvement as largely a public relations exercise aimed at fulfilling a management objective

Americans, on the other hand, are more likely to get involved because they are less likely to trust government. The unwillingness to leave it all to government drives citizen involvement to much higher levels in the US.

In *Continental Divide*, Martin Lipset explains how the different attitudes to government arose from the founding conditions of both countries: in the US it was the desire to escape British government rule; in Canada, it was just the opposite. Canadians unfamiliar with these differences are often demoralized by the lack of interest in citizen involvement in Canada, and puzzled why US models don't seem to work very well north of the border.

Introduce civics into public education

Introducing high school students to the machinery of local government would help to foster an interest in how government works and how it might work better.

In Canada there is none of this. Young people are more apt to be familiar with the sex life of slugs or the geography of Antarctica than the workings of their own government.

Teaching citizen involvement practices from other countries and group decision-making practices from traditional societies would help young people imagine a role for themselves as active citizens. Integrating this theory with real community projects would introduce students to the flesh and blood of citizenship.

Having a knowledge of democratic institutions' rights and responsibilities is more than a nice idea. It is essential to citizen participation and to the emergence of progressive states. In *Civic Literacy: How Informed Citizens Make Democracy Work,* Henry Milner demonstrates a strong correlation between voter turnout and basic political knowledge.

He also demonstrates a strong correlation between civic literacy and the *sustainable* welfare state that is found in Sweden, the Netherlands, Finland, and Denmark.

Revive the concept of citizen owners

In *Reinventing Government or Reinventing Ourselves: The Role of Citizen Owners in Making a Better Government,* Hindy Schachter tells the little-known story of the Bureau of Municipal Research (BMR) in New York City.

From 1907 to 1914 the BMR carried out a remarkable experiment in citizen participation based on the metaphor of citizens as "owners" of government. Heavily influenced by Frederick Taylor's theories of scientific management, the BMR promoted more efficient and more responsive government by encouraging a well-informed, active citizenry. As owners, citizens were expected to take an interest in government and how well government used their money. They were also expected to become active participants who set the civic agenda and addressed the needs of the whole civic enterprise.

Unfortunately, this view was too much for the Rockefeller philanthropies that funded the BMR. In 1914 they pulled financial support and the BMR vanished. Today mainstream institutions, government, and the press promote the view of citizens as passive consumers of public goods, who respond to agendas set by a managerial elite. In their view, citizens should know their place and properly concern themselves with meeting their own private needs, leaving public needs to professionals.

Schachter proposes a scheme for civic reform that begins where the BMR left off. She calls for an annual report on the operations of government agencies that would be written in plain English with lots of visuals. This report would be mailed to every citizen. It would include an explanation of why people should care about the document, a list of goals for agencies, an independent assessment of accomplishments, a description of problems encountered and solutions tried, and an explanation of any need to revise plans. Interested citizens could receive more detailed agency reports. Citizens who read these more detailed reports would be invited to attend neighborhood meetings with high-level agency executives to discuss government performance and performance indicators.

Put electoral reform on the public agenda

Many activists believe that electing "better" people is the best way to achieve progressive change. The main reason this book downplays electoral politics is that it limits citizen involvement to voting every few years. The rest of the time bureaucrats and elected politicians call the shots. Nevertheless, electing progressive people, and electoral reform offer many opportunities for improvement.

If you want to win an election, learn how. If you want to win an election, buy a copy of *Taking Back Politics* by Cathy Allen and follow the advice on running a campaign. Surprisingly few people involved in electoral politics know how to win an election.

Introduce partial proportional representation. Since the Second World War most western countries have updated and reformed their election systems. Canada and the US are the exceptions. The main obstacle to reform is politicians who do not want to change the system that elected them. The most recommended reform is to elect some people to public office through a proportion of the popular vote. In this system, parties with 10 percent of the vote would get 10 percent of the seats set aside for proportional representation. At present, a party that gets 10 percent of the vote usually elects no one. That leaves many voters out in the cold; either they vote for unattractive front-runners or they waste their vote. The unfairness of the winner-takes-all election system does not have to continue. There is now sufficient experience in numerous democracies to draft a fair and effective proportional system for governments in Canada and the US.

Introduce iron-clad limits for campaign expenses. Much tighter restrictions on campaign expenses are needed in both Canada and the US to prevent elites from buying elections with large advertising budgets. Loophole-free reporting provisions are also needed to reveal the ultimate source of every candidate's campaign funds.

Publish candidates' bios. One helpful reform would be a requirement of government to fact-check and publish candidates' resumés. This would give voters something more concrete than election promises to consider when deciding how to vote. Providing resumés would be part of the way candidates applied for the job of representing voters. There is a good reason why employers pay so much attention to resumés and references from job seekers. The best predictor of future performance is past performance.

Part-time politicians. Part-time politicians are common in Europe. Instead of a few full-time politicians making all the decisions, a much larger number of part-time politicians look after specific parts of government while holding a regular job. This spreads the task of governing over many more people and prevents the centralization of power in a few key people.

6.7 GRASSROOTS WILT 7 Counteractive Tactics

Those who oppose citizens initiatives have become more sophisticated as citizens groups have learned how to press their demands. Skeptical governments and self-serving corporations have devised numerous PR maneuvers for killing citizen initiatives. Here are some of them.

General tactics for countering a campaign

- Quietly assure insiders and partners that there is nothing to worry about.
- Privately discredit campaign facts and research.
- Publicly ignore the campaign or brush it off as a nuisance.
- If pressed, discredit the campaign as unrealistic, extremist, or self-interested.

Specific counteractive tactics

Make it difficult for people to become involved. Use the clock. Hold important meetings when it is difficult for people to attend. Schedule lengthy one-way presentations while holding off questions from the press and the public till the end, when the press has left, people are tired, or the room has to be vacated. Set time limits on individual statements from the public, but allow people at the front of the room to go on at length.

"Who elected you?" This little question often throws activists off balance. Walter Robinson of the Canadian Taxpayers Federation replies, "My answer is simple: Nobody elected us. We're a group of people exercising their democratic right to freedom of expression.

If you don't like it, to be very blunt, exercise yours and show us where our ideas are wrong."

"You're invited to a stakeholders' meeting." This could be a genuine effort to work out an agreement that satisfies everyone, but often it is a device to keep your group quiet by throwing you a few crumbs. Kim Bobo, Jackie Kendall, and Steve Max, the authors of *Organizing for Social Change: The Midwest Academy Manual for Activists,* suggest testing the intent of the invitation by agreeing to take part, on the understanding that you will make public everything that occurs at meetings, and continue to pursue a public campaign focused on your objectives.

"It could affect your funding." Treat this as a threat. Non-profits and citizens groups know that if they take a controversial stand, funding could disappear and their very existence threatened.

A version of this counteractive tactic is embedded in law. Both Canada and the US place severe restrictions on the political activity a group can undertake in exchange for granting charity status and the ability to issue tax receipts. Without the ability to issue tax receipts it is more difficult to raise funding, so the threat of affecting funding becomes: "It could affect your charitable status."

Divide and conquer. The divide and conquer strategy has many variants, including:

—Dividing a large issue into many small ones. This may be a genuine attempt to address an issue that is too large to handle in one chunk. On the other hand, it could be a way of generating many different focuses and many small battles that drain people's energy. A variation of this tactic is to create fake concerns that distract activists from the main event.

—Dividing the discussion with stakeholders. This may be a legitimate attempt to resolve an issue before positions are hardened. On the other hand, it may be a divide-and-conquer tactic to visit and talk with various interested groups separately.

—"Your group is reasonable. Can't we just deal with you?" This again may be a legitimate attempt to find a link to the grassroots. On the other hand, it could be an attempt to divide and conquer by excluding your allies. Counteractive professionals recognize it is easy to split the opposition into radicals, idealists, and realists and then get these factions fighting amongst themselves.

Fake process. Fake process usually involves holding a big meeting of stakeholders or "the community." Such meetings can help people on different sides see one another's point of view. On the other hand, they give an impression of bottom-up decision making while preserving a top-down process. Usually the idea is to have many small group discussions and then to synthesize the results of all these discussions. But there is rarely enough time to consider the facts, different perspectives, or the consequences of different courses of action, so it's impossible to reach well-considered conclusions. Participants, left with a frustrating muddle, are often quite happy to let the conveners sort out the mess.

Fake citizens groups. This is a corporate PR trick. A corporation will create one or more fake grassroots groups with big budgets to represent and lobby for its interests. The most common are fake environmental groups, sometimes called greenwash or astroturf organizations. These groups became so numerous that Greenpeace decided to list them in a book, along with information on who they actually represented.

Fake lawsuits. A "strategic lawsuit against political participation" or SLAPP is a nasty corporate tactic designed to scare off citizen opposition by raising the specter of financial loss and huge legal fees. The SLAPP is usually withdrawn before anything goes to court. Citizens should not be scared off by a SLAPP, but should seek help from a lawyer who will provide pro bono assistance.

Stack the public meeting. With this trick a single interest, often a business interest, brings a crowd of extra people to a public hearing. A corporation, for instance, might encourage employees, posing as ordinary citizens, to attend a public hearing it wants to influence.

Stacking is common at hearings for proposed land use projects. Typically, the project developer will register early for a group of friends and associates to speak at the hearing. This group will speak first, setting the tone of the meeting and often running out the clock before any citizen can speak. Usually another meeting will be scheduled to hear the remaining speakers. But many citizens who have wasted hours on the first round will decide to pass on the second. Active citizens can counter this tactic by asking their supporters to get their names on the speakers list quickly.

A variation on stacking the meeting is to have people submit questions in writing rather than verbally from an audience microphone. With written questions it is easy for those at the front of the room to stack the deck by ignoring questions that are slanted in the wrong direction.

"Let's negotiate." If your group has no real power, there is little reason why anyone would want to negotiate with you. This is usually a counteractive tactic aimed at delaying and dividing. Real negotiating comes at the end of a campaign, when you have demonstrated your power and a target hopes to change your behavior by giving you what you want.

Give the impression of doing something while doing nothing. This is another delaying tactic. Ask for a delivery date. Don't accept a date that is months in the future unless there is a good reason to do so.

"We've been working with the community." Again, this might be a legitimate response. It is not when "the community" is a collection of people who support what a government or corporation is trying to do. By giving official status to some groups while ignoring others, decision makers marginalize the opposition.

"We'd like to appoint you to a board, a commission, a working group." This might be a genuine attempt to get your input, or it might be an old-fashioned way to get your silence. This technique also serves to eat up the time of unpaid activists. Even the keenest have a limited amount of spare time; if it is spent with bureaucrats it won't be spent organizing an opposition.

Co-optive carrots and economic sticks. A co-optive carrot is an offer of a job, of contract work, or of project funding. A common economic stick is a threat of layoffs. Because layoffs have become commonplace, corporations can easily scare employees into cooperative behavior and into opposing outside activists who are working to get a company to improve safety or stop polluting.

"I love to help you, but I'm the wrong person." This trick is designed to present you with a fog rather than a clear target. You can go round in circles with no one willing to admit to being the right person.

"Yes, if you can get everyone's support." A government favorite. Let's say you are dealing with a number of groups with different positions on an issue. If you try to get everyone's support, you waste huge amounts of time meeting with people who have no reason to negotiate with you. Meanwhile, government, which *can* negotiate an agreement, has gotten rid of you and can point to your failure as a reason to maintain the status quo.

Withholding and other tricks with information. Honest governments put all important documents on their websites.

Governments that are less forthcoming:

- make information hard to get so you will give up and go away
- make information expensive so you cannot afford it, often by charging for public interest Freedom of Information requests
- provide misleading information
- provide information at the last minute so you have no time to respond,
- provide large quantities of useless information so you will waste huge amounts of time sorting through junk.

How to counter counteractive tactics

The Environment Information Network suggests that activists facing counteractive tactics take the following steps:

1. Be observant of interactions and of who may be maneuvering behind the scenes. Develop strategic responses that target people at the top.

2. Label a counteractive tactic as soon as it becomes apparent. When you label a tactic publicly it loses its power.

3. Don't allow bureaucrats to identify you as a troublemaker, a crank, a government hobbyist, a chronic volunteer, or somebody who is not worth listening to because you don't have "x" number of constituents behind you. All of these are ad hominem attacks (attacks on the person). They are not legitimate in any forum. Respond in a cool, businesslike manner and insist on forgoing ad hominem attacks in favor of addressing the problem.

6.8   GRASSROOTS WILT 8 Technocratic Control

Daniel Yankelovich's *Coming to Public Judgment: Making democracy work in a complex world* is one of the best books on practical public engagement.

Yankelovich begins the book with an attack on the culture of technical control in government, which turns over the bulk of important policy making to a tiny group of experts on the assumption that they know better than the public which is ill-informed and apathetic. Yankelovich argues that the growing gap between experts and citizens is undermining the foundations of democracy.

Experts should not displace citizens. Experts may be able to address technical questions, but only the public and its leaders are capable of addressing questions of value.

Yankelovich condemns another aspect of technical control: the view that polling is a reliable guide to public opinion. As the father of modern polling and a former partner in a large polling firm, Yankelovich argues that most polling results are highly volatile "mass opinion" that can change dramatically with slight changes in the wording of polling questions. They are volatile because people have not taken the time to consider the consequences of various positions on an issue. When they spend time to "come to public judgment," their responses become stable. Only then are their views a reliable basis for public policy.

Yankelovich spends most of his book detailing how the people can come to public judgment. He identifies three stages in the process:

1. Consciousness raising

2. Working-through

3. Resolution

In the first stage, people become aware of the issue principally through publicity in the mass media. The first stage is well understood. Citizen and advocacy groups regularly raise important issues using various techniques to access the mass media. These are covered in detail in Chapter 9. According to Yankelovich, a number of factors speed up consciousness raising:

- A clear, concrete presentation of the issue

- News events that visually dramatize the issue

- Credible sources who call for action

- Advocacy groups who generate lots of publicity about the issue

- Personal consequences that increase people's interest in the issue (Consciousness of AIDS increased when it became clear it was more than just a problem amongst homosexuals.)

The second stage – working-through – is murky and difficult. Many second stage problems arise from the mass media that was so helpful in the first stage. The second stage becomes difficult when people receive contradictory information, do not receive sufficient or adequate choices for action, and do not understand the consequences of various choices. It also becomes more difficult when the mass media diverts people's attention before they have time to come to grips with an issue.

Experts create second-stage problems by providing contradictory information, by trying to own issues in a way that displaces the public, and by quietly imposing their own values in a way that displaces values held by the public. Experts also distort policy issues by emphasizing quantifiable technical variables (their area of expertise) in a way that displaces qualitative variables important to the public.

Working-through can take anywhere from "minutes to centuries." One simple form of working-through involves the second thoughts people have when they are given time to consider an emotionally packed issue.

A second form is about getting used to new realities, such as the vulnerability of oil supplies that became apparent during the 1970s. The most common form involves people coming to grips with conflicting feelings, opinions, attitudes, and values. Because this can take time, the main problem at stage two is finding time.

Yankelovich provides a number of rules to help leaders with the difficulties at stages 2 and 3.

Rules for working-through and resolution.

Do not depend on experts to present issues. On any given issue the experts and the public will be out of sync.

Learn what the public's main preoccupation is and address it before any other facet of the issue.

Let the public know someone is listening and cares.

Limit to two or three the number of issues people must attend to at any given time.

Help people move beyond quick and easy answers.

Provide choices to help the process of working-through.

Remember that leaders must highlight the value components of choices.

When two conflicting values are both important to the public, try to preserve elements of each.

Allow extra time to break down obstacles.

This short summary cannot do justice to Yankelovich's book. Interested readers should search out a copy of his prescription for doing democracy better.

In *The Trajectory of Change*, Michael Albert looks at what is required for large campaigns such as the anti-globalization movement to make progress. He argues that many large campaigns have stalled because the number of people involved has "plateaued." The anti-globalization effort can mobilize several thousand people for a street demonstration during meetings of the World Trade Organization, the World Bank, or the International Monetary Fund. But that's it. The numbers are not growing. For a movement to take off it needs to spread from a few to many. Most movements today are physically contained by government and symbolically contained by the mass media. To make any progress under these conditions, the number of people involved needs to become much larger.

Presently, it is the usual suspects who do the planning, and the usual suspects who show up at demonstrations – the same people every time. Albert compares the usual suspects to the front-runners in a race who pull away, leaving everyone else behind. Leaving the bulk of potential supporters behind is counterproductive. To build a successful social movement, front-runners need to bring others along; they need to engage the disengaged and turn bystanders into active participants.

It is easier for the front-runners to relate to a small and supportive subculture that agrees with them, but to build a movement they need to talk to people who don't agree and people who have never given their issue any thought. As Michael Albert says:

> *Suppose, for example, that we are on a major campus like the football-focused one in State College, Pennsylvania, where I recently spoke. If our core movement of a couple of hundred folks spends all its time relating together and to people very like themselves, and almost none of its time going into sports bars and fraternities and all the other campus venues where 40,000 other students congregate, how are we going to become a majority project? . . It takes great courage, commitment, and knowledge to become radical on such a campus and then work for and go to a demonstration miles away. . . But there is another step in movement building, and it also takes courage: to become adept at going into that local sports bar and drumming up a conversation over and over, with the folks who we need to win over to our movement.*

Hoping to make progress in a sports bar sounds overly optimistic. But Albert has a point: we need to move our conversations into new venues. And these conversations cannot amount to proselytizing from a superior position; they must be friendly discussions that gently frame current events from an activist perspective.

We also need new ways for people to get involved. Committed front-runners are willing to travel to far-off demonstrations and engage in physical confrontation that may lead to arrest. But less committed people balk at this kind of strong action, and people with jobs or kids usually can't afford a lacuna for travel and incarceration. If front-runners care about making progress, they need to spend as much time strategizing over the involvement of ordinary people as they do over their own involvement.

6.10   **GRASSROOTS WILT 10** Collective Action Catch-22

Dennis Chong begins his award-winning book *Collective Action and the Civil Rights Movement* with an important question. What determines whether rational individuals will participate in public-spirited collective action? To answer this question he turns to game theory. In particular, Chong argues that collective action faces a multiplayer prisoner's dilemma problem. When it comes to acquiring a public good, rational people will decline to participate, preferring instead a "free ride," since they will be able to obtain the public good whether they participate or not. But this is ultimately unworkable. The collective result of everyone not participating is complete failure.

To get around the problem, Chong rightly argues that people must be given some incentive to participate beyond the public good itself. When social and psychological factors are brought into play the prisoner's dilemma game turns into an assurance game, where people find it in their interest to participate if others do so as well. Thus:

— People participate out of a sense of obligation to friends, family, and associates. They also respond to a sense of decency and fair play and a desire to avoid damaging their reputation if they appear unwilling to help.

— People participate if there is evidence of success, so leaders should aim for a series of small victories over the short term rather than focus on the big victory down the road. Even symbolic victories are important. To help followers weather early storms and lack of success, leaders should frame the smallest success as a victory. They should cheer any hint the opposition is giving in to demands. In the absence of any evidence, movement leaders must convince potential followers that, despite appearances, those in power are pliable and will eventually give in to political pressure. For their part, those in power will try to stonewall activists to deny them the victories that will breathe life into their movement. The result of these strategies is a contest of wills in which each side tries to outlast the other.

—People are more likely to participate if there is evidence of lots of other people participating. This presents social movement groups with a catch-22. They can only succeed if many people participate, but people will only participate if they see evidence of success and the participation of others.

Overcoming the catch-22 requires a small band of leaders and unconditional supporters. Chong writes:

> Leaders become involved irrespective of the degree of success and the level of mobilization previously established by the movement. Followers, on the other hand, join collective action only in response to success and the existing levels of mobilization. In other words, leaders act autonomously, while followers jump on the bandwagon, as well as respond to the contagion of the movement.

Overcoming the catch-22 also depends on creating the impression that others are joining in the effort. Those on the other side, of course, try to create the opposite impression.

Rising expectations also boost participation. The great English, American, French, and Russian revolutions took place when the material conditions of life were actually improving. Movement leaders can take advantage of this by holding up an enviable standard as something everyone should rightfully enjoy.

Finally, a mobilizing frame encourages participation – see Appendix 3. It's not so much the facts of economic deprivation, inequality, injustice, and official incompetence that mobilize people as their perceptions of these problems. If the problems are viewed as inevitable or rooted in individual failings, there is no reason to demand systemic change. Not surprisingly, wealthy elites – including those who own the mass media – tend to "blame the victim" because they do not wish to contribute to systemic changes that would benefit the less fortunate.

Disposing of blame-the-victim propaganda is a necessary precursor to systemic change. In the civil rights movement, for example, blacks first had to be persuaded not to blame themselves for their inferior status.

Grassroots wilt is a scourge that goes virtually unnoticed. Because it receives so little attention, people have come to view citizen involvement as unusual, and citizen action as a waste of time. Activists and those who are interested in the larger project of strengthening civil society need to pay far more attention to its causes. Even a little attention could have enormous consequences by drawing out those who have a natural interest in public business, those who wish to spend less time at a regular job, and those of the baby boomer generation who are leaving the workforce but want to do something that will make a difference.

The shadowy group Guerrilla Media (guerrillamedia.org) posted these fake official notices on trees around Vancouver, upsetting residents until they realized the notices were actually making fun of City Hall. The people behind Guerrilla Media are real troublemakers.

CHAPTER 7

Strategic Action

THE MOST EFFECTIVE ACTIVISTS think, plan, and act strategically. Inexperienced activists make the mistake of focusing only on stopping things. Their only action is reaction. Duff Conacher of Democracy Watch observes, "All they do is maintain the status quo and they actually lose in the long run, because the rules never change and there are all sorts of things they're not stopping."

Strategic action is necessary in situations where an opponent blocks the way to an objective. In such cases, smart activists use strategic thinking to identify where an opponent is vulnerable, and then try to figure out how to exploit that vulnerability. They also use strategic thinking to solve problems before they happen, coolly examining the pros and cons of various moves in order to identify the best course of action.

7.1   Creating a Strategy

Creating a strategy for a public interest campaign involves:

- defining goals and intermediate and short-term objectives,
- identifying opponents,
- carrying out a SWOT analysis,
- imagining and playing scenarios,
- identifying primary and secondary targets,
- identifying allies,
- deciding what resources are required (salaries, expenses, other),
- devising tactics, and
- drawing up an action timetable.

This is a loopy not a linear process. So, you might define an objective up-front but realize later that resources are inadequate to achieve this goal or that there is no clear target. Thus you will need to loop back to redefine the objective.

Defining goals and objectives. Your goals are the broad results you wish to achieve over the long term. Objectives are what you want to accomplish more immediately. Your objectives should follow naturally from your goals. They help you reach your goal. If the goal is winning the war, an objective might be winning a particular battle.

If you lose sight of your goals and objectives, everything goes haywire. Consider a project to address the problems of global capitalism; it leads to a street protest, which brings about a police attack on protesters. A protracted inquiry into police brutality then sidetracks the whole project, obscuring the message of the protest and trumping its main objective.

Identifying opponents and obstacles. What stands in the way of reaching your objective? Who can make the necessary changes? Who specifically do you need to influence? If you are trying to bring about changes to government policy or legislation, you will want to avoid making incorrect assumptions about how government works, who is responsible, or what is the most effective route for bringing about change.

Carrying out a SWOT analysis. It's easier to make choices after identifying strengths, weaknesses, opportunities, and threats. A SWOT analysis can be applied to a position, an idea, an individual, or an organization. Consider a SWOT analysis for your group as well as for your target. See also 9.2 "Creating Messages."

Imagining and playing scenarios. Strategic thinking is often described as reflective dialogue about the future so that you can avoid pitfalls and exploit opportunities. One way to do this is by imagining how events will play out, then devising effective responses. Future scenarios may be framed as "what if" questions. Let's say you are planning to hike up a mountain. The sun is shining, so you prepare gear and clothing based on a default scenario that assumes an easy hike in fine weather. But your preparations will change if you consider "what if" questions. "What if fog makes it difficult to see?" "What if it snows?" "What if someone sprains their ankle?" Good scenarios require informed imagination. If it's not informed, you can waste energy on the improbable. If it's not fueled by imagination, you can be blindsided.

Identifying primary and secondary targets. If your group can-not itself deliver a public good, you must be able to identify a decision maker or primary target who can. Campaigns directed at getting a target to do something usually require negotiation, cam-paigning, and confrontation. These tactics work best on people who are elected. Hired bureaucrats and appointed officials are more resistant.

You should also identify one or more secondary targets. These are people who will cooperate with you, who have some power over the primary target. Secondary targets might be regulatory offi-cials, important customers, or politicians from a more senior level of government.

Identifying allies. If you can't influence a decision maker on your own, are there others who can help? When groups with similar interests create strategic alliances, they are much more likely to achieve their goals. The tendency for groups to compete for funds and influence merely serves the opposition.

Allies may also be sympathetic insiders. Citizens need intelligence to make the right moves.

The best intelligence comes from inside organizations that can influence the success of your project. Let's suppose your goal is to change government policy. Reading government reports will pro-vide some useful information. But talking to bureaucrats will provide new information and a quick rundown on attitudes inside government. A sympathetic senior bureaucrat who under-stands your project can provide the most help. Finding such a person will help you make all the right moves.

Devising tactics. Tactics are the action part of a strategy. Generating good tactical alternatives requires creative thinking.

Choosing which tactic to use, on the other hand, requires a knowledge of what works in a particular context. It also requires some consideration of what will be good, interesting, or exciting for the group.

—Does the key decision maker agree with your objectives and your solutions? If so, cooperative tactics make sense.

—Does the decision maker agree with your objectives but not your solutions? If so, consider tactics focused on persuasion and negotiation.

—Does the decision maker completely disagree with both your objectives and your solutions? Then confrontation may be the only option.

Most campaigns include many different kinds of tactics.Tactics differ in what they try to accomplish. They can aim to:

- win an objective by giving the other side something it wants – credit, votes, support,
- win an objective by depriving or threatening to deprive the other side of something it wants – credibility, respect, money, labor, employment,
- build public support in the media or build the support of allies or secondary targets,
- show a target the size and concern of your constituency, or
- build the morale of your group.

To evaluate a tactic, try to answer the following questions:

Is the tactic aimed at achieving a clear objective?
Is the tactic focused on a primary or secondary target?
Is it based on a thorough understanding of the target?
Is the tactic in tune with other things that are happening?
Does it demand action?
Is your group comfortable with the tactic?
Has your group exhausted all options for cooperation and negotiation? Confrontation should be a last resort.
If it is confrontational, does it respect Alinsky's Rules for Radicals? See 10.2 "Rules for Radicals."

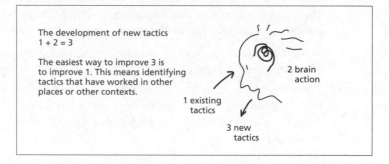

The development of new tactics
1 + 2 = 3

The easiest way to improve 3 is to improve 1. This means identifying tactics that have worked in other places or other contexts.

2 brain action

1 existing tactics

3 new tactics

Drawing up a detailed action timetable. Your timetable should be a multilevel chart with start and completion dates for everything you want to do, as well as start and completion dates for all significant external events such as voter registration. Strategies that involve winning something from a target usually begin with opening a line of communication with the target, and then move on to action meetings. See 8.3 "Hold an action meeting".

7.2   Creating Effective Strategies

Take the initiative. Too often citizens groups simply react to the actions of government or corporations. Randy Shaw, author of *The Activist's Handbook: A Primer for the 1990s & Beyond,* says this is the main mistake of citizens groups and the main mechanism by which the grassroots is marginalized. Reacting is about knee-jerk responses. Strategic thinking is about taking the initiative.

Try on their shoes. To begin thinking strategically try putting yourself in the shoes of those you want to influence. Try to antici-pate how targets will respond to various tactics. This means you have to know your targets well enough to gauge how they will react. For some subjects and some businesses, accurate anticipation may require simulation.

Live off the land. Strategic thinkers make use of what is available. For instance, they like to devise ways of linking their issue to breaking news in order to access the mass media.

Beware of the media's love of confrontation. If your strategy requires cooperation, be careful about attracting media attention. Many journalists look for stories rooted in conflict, error, and injustice. They may impose a confrontational agenda that can actually make cooperation more difficult.

Consider "win-win" strategies. Win-win strategies are the best strategies because both sides come out ahead. They require par-ticipants to discard fixed positions, focus on interests they have in common, and invent options for mutual gain. Participants should try to see themselves on the same side instead of on different sides.

Many land development projects result in pitched battles between developers and residents. This can be avoided if everyone focuses on the potential for mutual gain. In one Vancouver project, local residents supported rather than opposed a hospital extension after working out a deal that had the hospital create a pocket park suitable for both residents and patients.

Developing options for mutual gain requires some practice. For help with this approach see the literature on conflict resolution, including *Getting to Yes* by Roger Fisher and William Ury, and *The Magic of Dialogue* by Daniel Yankelovich.

Consider can't-lose strategies. Can't-lose actions give you a win no matter how your adversary responds. It's well worth the time to invent or identify can't-lose opportunities.

Let's suppose a citizen's group is trying to improve the system by which people are elected to a city council. The group decides to ask council for money to encourage people to vote in the polls with the lowest voter turnout. If council says yes, the group can improve voter turnout. If council says no, the group can reveal council's lack of interest in a fair and representative electoral process.

Consider a markets campaign. A markets campaign focuses on secondary targets, usually an opponent's most important corporate or institutional customers. It tries to get these customers to stop purchasing from an opponent that refuses to improve its social or environmental practices.

A markets campaign protects forests

Greenpeace and the Rainforest Action Network used a markets campaign to force Canadian forestry companies to adopt ecological logging methods. They mailed letters to 5,000 buyers, large retailers and companies such as Kinko's and Xerox. Retailers started canceling orders. Next Ikea came on board and other companies began to follow. The most resistant was Home Depot. The Network decided to demonstrate at Home Depot stores. At one time in 1999 activists were busy at over a hundred stores, making speeches with megaphones, giving critical store tours, even commenting on wood purchases while hanging from the rafters over checkout counters. Finally Home Depot agreed to purchase only wood that met the standards of the Forest Stewardship Council.

A markets campaign goes after pesticides

On a smaller scale, Sharon Labchuk decided to use a markets campaign to draw attention to massive increases in the use of chemical sprays on Prince Edward Island. She produced pamphlets entitled "How to Protect Your Family from Pesticide Poisoning While Visiting Prince Edward Island or What the PEI Government Won't Tell You in the Tourist Brochures" and handed them out to tourists waiting for the ferry to PEI.

Consider "tip-it" strategies. Strategic thinkers stress the importance of deciding *when* to act. There is no sense beating your head against a brick wall if no one will respond. Activists who can identify the approach of a "tipping point" are able to take advantage of favorable timing to achieve their goals.

Take the problem of drug abuse. When the US film *Traffic* garnered attention and Oscar nominations, activists found it was an opportune time to push hard for a new approach to drug abuse. *Traffic* and its British predecessor showed a wider public what experts had known for a long time: the war on drugs was an expensive failure. Newspapers started writing more stories favoring harm reduction over police enforcement. Lining up with the left-wing harm-reduction advocates were right-wing think tanks alarmed by wasteful government expenditure. Communities began demanding an end to break-and-enters by a relatively small number of addicts desperate for quick cash. In 2002 the time was right in Vancouver for a new approach to drug addiction.

Even when the time is right, advocates for change need to push hard to reach the tipping point on controversial issues to overcome the cautiousness and the deadweight inertia of government. Opportunities can evaporate before anything is achieved if movement is too slow. One of the ways activists pushed government on harm reduction in Vancouver was to open their own safe-injection site without government approval.

Engage youth. Resolving large-scale social problems often takes many years, so it is smart to focus on educating or involving children. Working to include public interest material and progressive perspectives in the school curriculum pays off down the road. Today, many young people are rabid environmentalists thanks to a public school system that has sensitized students to environmental issues.

Meat the teacher

In Britain, animal rights activists brought video documentaries showing animals being slaughtered into the classroom. It turned thousands of kids into instant vegetarians.

Encouraging youth activism is a strategic way of improving media access, because young people at the center of a story will almost always attract media attention. What interests youth is considered new and topical and therefore worth covering.

To engage youth, arrange for youth to talk to youth – particularly those who have pertinent first-hand experience. Young people will listen to peers, while preaching adults will put them to sleep. The easiest way to arrange for youth to talk to youth is to arrange to do it in schools.

Prepare for the long haul. Press your case, but recognize government tends to move at a snail's pace. If your objective is a major new government initiative or a policy shift, rapid movement may be difficult. Groups that think strategically don't wear themselves out by trying to push a government process beyond its speed limit. They plan for the long haul. Less sophisticated groups give up. John Gardiner, founder of Common Cause, is emphatic about the importance of sustained action. "The first basic rule we have learned is that an effective instrument of citizen action must be a continuing effort. One of the basic failings of citizen effort is the unpredictable waxing and waning of enthusiasm."

Lock up gains with legislation. If your goal is progressive legislation, push for legislation without delay at the conclusion of a campaign, Progress made through media advocacy and direct contact with politicians can easily evaporate when the media and politicians shift their attention to other topics.

7.3 Spawning

Spawning is the practice of giving birth to organizations, practices, and productions (events, workshops, and campaigns) that are independent and sustainable. Spawning is a strategic move aimed at spreading what you are doing in one organization in one place to other organizations in other places. Some examples:

—An existing group might spawn new groups to do the same work in new places.

—An existing group with skilled organizers might create a web resource that will spawn effective organizing practices.

—An existing group might establish an annual conference that will spawn initiatives in line with its own work.

Narrowly focused spawning makes sense for small groups because it provides a large benefit for time invested. By creating a new public interest operation and allowing others to take it over, a small group can extend the efforts of a few members far beyond their actual involvement.

Incubation

Spawning usually requires some sort of incubation to prevent a new enterprise from expiring. An incubator provides a project or organization with resources until it can manage on its own. Business incubators are facilities that allow businesses to share resources as a low-cost means to getting started. You may have a non-profit incubator in your community. In the US contact the National Council of Nonprofit Associations.

An organization gives birth. Existing organizations often spawn new organizations and productions, then incubate them inside their own walls with contacts, equipment, and knowledgeable staff.

A grant gives birth. People who write convincing grant applications can be inordinately fecund – even more so if they know where the money is and where they can find people with impressive credentials to support their applications.

Sometimes grant-seeking groups have to apply under the wing of a mother organization with a track record to dispel worries granters may have about credibility and accountability. Grants are not the only source of money for spawning; others are bequests, endowments, and contracts.

A gathering gives birth. Organizing a meeting of people with a common interest can often give birth to something new – even if it is only a new network that helps everyone stay in touch and share information. Conferences seem to be fertile ground in themselves, spawning the formation of new groups, which in turn spawn their own organizations and productions.

The British group This Land is Ours emerged from a discussion following a conference on direct action in Oxford in 1994 at which several people expressed the need to go on the offensive, to start demanding what they did want, rather than protesting what they didn't.

A workshop gives birth. When it comes to training activists, workshops seem to reach more people than books do. That's why organizations with progressive objectives invariably establish regular training workshops that put novices with experienced people who can inspire them and set them on the right course.

Networks nurture spawning. Those who study epidemics, social networks, and viral marketing place a great deal of importance on the role of "hubs" – people who know and interact with a lot of other people. Not surprisingly these "hubs" nurture newly spawned organizations, practices, and productions by bringing many people to otherwise small and isolated efforts. For more on spreading ideas through social networks see *The Anatomy of Buzz* by Emanuel Rosen and *The Tipping Point* by Malcolm Gladwell.

7.4   Workshops

Conducting a workshop is one way to encourage spawning. By creating an opportunity for experienced people to pass on what they know, workshops build confidence and a will to act. They also inform people who might buy, but will never read a manual for effective citizen action.

This is not the place to go into the details of running a successful training workshop, but a few points are worth making.

A workshop when? Workshops are most appropriate when they focus on group learning and learning by doing. If you simply want to convey information or move people to act, giving a speech might make more sense. Workshops also seem to work best when people taking the workshop have the same background and level of experience.

Give the essential information in different forms. Identify a few things you want everybody to take away from the workshop. Repeat these essentials in five different ways. Say them; write them; summarize them; put them in an exercise; ask a question about them; tell a story about them.

Real-life exercises and role-plays. In a real-life exercise, two or three people get together to tackle some real-life task such as writing a headline for a news release or developing a campaign strategy. Workshop organizers move from group to group providing on-the-spot help. Results are then reviewed and discussed.

To set up a role-play, workshop organizers create a simple background scenario, ideally one they have encountered themselves. Different people are assigned different roles and asked to resolve some real-life problem. Adults will usually balk at role-playing for fear of looking silly, but afterwards will feel the experience has been worthwhile. Don't set up role-plays for failure so you can make a point or look smart. Role-plays should build confidence. Debriefing should follow role-playing to identify what worked and what could have been better.

7.5   Coalitions

If you cannot achieve an objective on your own, establishing a partnership with another organization, or a coalition with many organizations, may make sense. A coalition builds power by focusing a number of organizations on a common objective. To set up either a coalition or a partnership, identify a group that can contribute something and ask to speak at its next executive meeting. After you have presented, distribute material outlining your objectives, program, and budget. A good way of getting agreement is to ask someone from the group you are approaching to help prepare your presentation.

To succeed, a coalition should be built around a single unifying objective. Participants need to have a clear set of expectations. They also need to agree on a decision-making process that recognizes different groups will contribute differently and to different degrees. A successful coalition with a major objective requires staff, an adequate budget, and a board made up of directors or senior members of participating groups. Coalition staff serve to build the coalition; they often meet with groups separately to identify common ground. Coalition staff spend a lot of time emphasizing that members do not have to agree on everything and that living with disagreements is necessary for the focus to remain on a common objective.

Coalitions seem to work best as temporary arrangements that lapse when an objective is achieved or discarded. Coalitions present all sorts of problems and opportunities. Before getting involved in one, review the advice in the latest edition of *Organizing for Social Change: The Midwest Academy Manual for Activists* by Kim Bobo, Jackie Kendall, and Steve Max.

7.6 The Strategy of Social Protest

In *The Strategy of Social Protest*, William Gamson looks at 53 citizens groups that operated in the US sometime between 1800 and 1945 to see what made them successful. He uses two measures for success: acceptance and advantages. Acceptance indicates the degree to which antagonists came to view a group as a voice for a legitimate set of interests. Advantages measures the degree to which the group achieved objectives or benefits. Gamson's findings suggest that some recent trends in organizational structure and strategy may be wrong-headed.

Bureaucratic group structure is an advantage. Bureaucratic groups scored about six times better on advantages and seven times better on acceptance. Gamson defines bureaucratic groups as having:

—a written constitution or charter that sets forth the goals of the organization;

—a formal list of members; and

—three levels of internal division such as executive director, board, rank and file.

Bureaucratic structure ensured that certain routine but critical tasks got done, and it helped groups survive long-term challenges. It should be noted that Gamson's conclusions apply to large groups. There is no need for bureaucratic structure for small, volunteer, citizens groups.

Centralization of power is an advantage. Groups with centralized power were twice as likely to earn new advantages as groups that were not centralized. Gamson attributes this to the "combat readiness" that comes from having a credible spokesperson or capable leader able to respond decisively when required to do so, without having to get the approval of a membership or a board. Today, many groups are moving in the opposite direction, trying to decentralize power in order to become more democratic.

Factionalism is a serious liability. Factionalism, resulting from the inability to deal with internal conflict, meant groups were about three times less able to win advantages and half as likely to be accepted. Factionalism was about three times more common in a decentralized group, because centralized power provided a way of dealing with internal conflict.

Unruliness works. Real or threatened strikes, boycotts, blockades, disruptive protests, verbal attacks and ridicule, and threats of violence achieved results. Groups that employed unruly tactics were twice as successful at securing advantages as those that did not.

Group size counts for acceptance. Groups with over 10,000 members were twice as likely to be accepted as groups with fewer than 10,000. However, the difference in size had little bearing on the ability of a group to win new advantages.

Avoid trying to displace antagonists. Groups that tried to displace, replace, or destroy antagonists were over six times less likely to be accepted, and over ten times less likely to achieve new advantages. According to Gamson, what gets in the way of ambitious challengers is targets of change unwilling to cooperate in their own demise. Sometimes the people are the problem, but more often it is better for activists to focus on fixing the problem rather than attacking the people involved.

CHAPTER 8

Direct Contact

A GREAT DEAL CAN BE ACCOMPLISHED by directly contacting those in power. People with a track record of getting things done do this all the time. They find out who is responsible, then pick up the phone and call them.

8.1   Contacting Government Bureaucrats

Despite their many deficiencies, western governments are still the most powerful allies of citizens interested in progressive change. Even when politicians seem bent on turning back the clock, government employees will often remain sympathetic to progressive citizen initiatives. The mistake many activists make is to think that activism belongs *outside* government. As a rule, if the goal is progressive legislation more than half of any activist initiative should focus *inside* government.

When working with government keep the following points in mind.

Issues requiring new legislation may take years to resolve. Some issues require patient persistence and many meetings with decision makers. The usual route for legislation is:

1. Obtain public support through coalition building and media advocacy.

2. Obtain bureaucratic support though meetings with senior bureaucrats.

3. Obtain political support through meetings with politicians.

In most cases one should not omit gaining bureaucratic support, since the first move of most politicians will be to ask a senior bureaucrat for an opinion on your request.

Figure out who is responsible. Different levels of government are responsible for different things, so there is no sense going after municipal government over a highway issue when it's a provincial or state responsibility. Identify the top politician who can begin the task of initiating the changes you desire. This might be a minister in Canada; for local government it might be a councilor who has assumed responsibility for your issue. Ideally you will find an advocate for your cause within government.

Phone the top person first. Try to get a meeting with the most senior person first, then work your way down to assistant top bureaucrats, their assistants, and so forth until you get a yes. Use the telephone rather than sending letters, faxes, and e-mail. Once you get a yes you can begin working your way back up the bureaucracy. Those at lower levels can bring your issue to the attention of those higher up or tell you how to go about doing it yourself.

Make yourself important. Top politicians and bureaucrats don't want to spend time meeting with nobodies. They will meet with people who are:
• well-connected
• have special expertise
• have a large constituency
• have the attention of the media

Your group may have to expend some energy making itself important. You can demonstrate a constituency by forming coalitions and partnerships, and by turning out lots of people for public events. You can acquire special expertise by doing research and by bringing in experts. You can earn the attention of the media by using any number of the media advocacy techniques described in Chapter 9.

8.2   Contacting Elected Politicians

In general, when contacting politicians be as specific and as brief as possible.

You will have the most impact if you focus on pending legislation. Draw from your own personal experience. Describe how it will affect you, your family, or your community.

Call elected politicians at the legislature or at their constituency offices, or send them e-mail or faxes. Government websites usually provide phone and fax numbers and e-mail links.

Write on personal letterhead, if you have it, and be sure to sign it.

Question legislators at public events. Keep questions short and to the point. Make sure your question is specific: "Will you make a public pledge to support this campaign reform effort?" Don't use a public forum as an occasion to argue, but don't let the legislator avoid answering the question.

To learn when key legislation is coming up in the US, visit *common cause.org, pirg.org,* or the websites of other government watchdogs.

In Canada, you can learn about pending legislation by subscribing to e-mail newsletters from groups trying to address specific issues.

Letter-writing bees

A pile of letters or faxes works a lot better than one. A sudden deluge of letters is especially effective for swaying local politicians.

Provincial, state, and federal politicians are less likely to respond because they are frequently the targets of PR campaigns in which hundreds of people are paid to write and telephone politicians about an issue. For more on this abysmal practice see *Who Will Tell the People: The Betrayal of American Democracy* by William Greider.

How to generate a flood of letters

To generate a flood of letters, set aside ten minutes for a letter-writing bee at group meetings, family gatherings, workshops, and public events.

Hand out pens and paper and ask everyone to write a letter on the spot. This addresses the main difficulty with letter writing: many people intend to do it but never get around to it.

Itemize the points a letter should cover.

Ask them to include a signature and a return address.

Don't ask them to mail their letters; it won't happen. Ask them to address an envelope and make a contribution to postage; then mail the letters yourself.

8.3 Meetings with Decision Makers

A straightforward way to address a problem is to ask those in charge to correct it. Before taking any other action, request a face-to-face meeting with the public servant, corporate officer, or politician responsible.

Decide your main and fallback demands. Your main demands should be requests for something of substance, such as dedicated bicycle lanes across bridges. In addition to your main demands, you should have several fallback demands. A fallback demand may be a more modest version of your main demand, or it may be a procedural demand such as a public inquiry or a study.

Hold an action meeting. Take the initiative by setting up an "action" meeting to put your demands to decision makers. Only invite people who have the power to grant your request. Organize the meeting on home ground in a place familiar to your delegation. Before the meeting, put your main demands in writing. Decide on various roles and an agenda and overall strategy for presenting your requests, then do a dress rehearsal. Just before the meeting, plan on a 30-minute huddle to confirm the agenda and ensure solidarity. The right tone for the meeting is firm, calm, and businesslike – not solicitous, not belligerent, not holier-than-thou, not wiser-than-thou. After the meeting, take some time for a postmortem to identify what worked and what didn't.

Be prepared for tricks.

Government and corporate managers take workshops on how to mollify hostile citizens. Look out for:

Last-minute substitutes. If the substitute has no power to grant your request, thank the substitute and adjourn the meeting.

A takeover. Don't let them take over. This is your meeting; your chair should run the meeting. Everyone should address the chair.

"We'll get back to you." Ask for a decision at the meeting. If this is impossible, request the official attend the next meeting of your organization or a special meeting with your executive. You need to be able to respond to the decision.

"We're all pals." Far too often citizens are co-opted by the friendly attention of important people. Stick to business. Preempt chummy chitchat and other co-optive tactics.

8.4   Public Meetings

Public meetings are one of the most common venues for bringing together citizens and decision makers. They are also one of the least productive. While many local governing bodies are required by law to hold public hearings, they bring out the worst in everybody.

- The physical set-up pits citizens against decision makers.

- Citizens make speeches in support of hardened positions. Little dialogue takes place.

- Because most hearings go on too long, only those who are really upset show up.

- Those with moderate positions rarely speak up for fear of being attacked by those with more extreme views.

- A large audience prompts grandstanding and point scoring on both sides. The presence of media makes matters worse.

Open houses have pros and cons. Because of the problems with public hearings, governments and business prefer open houses, with information displays and staff to answer questions. An open house makes an entire proposal continuously available, permits multiple conversations to take place simultaneously, and fits into people's busy schedules.

Citizens who hold strong views typically hate open houses. They claim open houses are a way of managing public input, of limiting the impact of embarrassing questions, and of neutralizing well-informed speakers.

A public meeting might be a better alternative if the only option remaining is confrontation. When citizens feel they are being managed through the use of open houses, they sometimes arrange their own public meeting. It won't contribute much to reasoned discussion, but it will improve oppositional solidarity and provide a way of identifying potential leaders.

Convert an open house into a public meeting. One way to put the powerful on the spot is to convert an open house into a public meeting. Let everyone know the time of conversion and invite the press. At the chosen time, move displays aside, bring out chairs, and invite the hosts to the front of the room to answer questions. A Vancouver group used this technique to address plans to run a rapid transit line through a natural ravine. Citizens rearranged the room, then invited their hosts to the front of the room. When the hosts remained at the back, someone said, "Let's turn our chairs around." This prompted the hosts to run out the door. One brave consultant finally came back, allowing a woman to ask how long they had taken to do their environmental impact study. When the consultant hedged, she kept asking, "How long?" Finally she got an answer: one day.

8.5   Accountability Sessions

An accountability session is a high-powered event in which activists put the screws on a local elected official. People from your constituency stand up and say why they expect the official to support a particular initiative. A panel of your leaders then makes specific demands, to which the official must respond. Accountability sessions are very effective when:

- lots of people fill the audience,
- people on the panel represent large groups or constituencies,
- the official is up for re-election and previously won by a narrow margin.

This tactic is mainly used in the US where officials are elected and have specific job descriptions. This means an accountability session becomes a forum for discussing whether the official is doing his or her job. In Canada, public officials are unelected civil servants. Canadian activists could use the tactic to target local politicians with specific portfolios. At present, they are more likely to invite local politicians to a conference. For details on holding an accountability session see the latest edition of *Organizing for Social Change: The Midwest Academy Manual for Activists* by Kim Bobo, Jackie Kendall, and Steve Max.

CHAPTER 9

Media Advocacy

I F YOU ARE JUST LOOKING for a little media attention, the short
summary 3.5 "Publicizing a Project" may be sufficient. This
chapter is about driving forward a public interest project by
putting your case forcefully in the media. To do this, activists have
developed a variety of techniques to earn – rather than purchase
– media coverage. Before we turn to these, we should look more
closely at media advocacy itself.

9.1   Media Advocacy Does a Lot

It sets the agenda. Citizen action that is largely invisible has no
effect on anyone other than participants The purpose of media
advocacy is to keep the spotlight focused on your issue, says
Lawrence Wallach, author of *Media Advocacy and Public Health.*

It drives government. Most politicians and bureaucrats wish
media did not drive government. But it does. When Vancouver
City Hall politicians and bureaucrats received a draft of the
Citizens Handbook, the precursor to this book, they marked up
the section on getting media attention with a blizzard of blue, red,
yellow, and black pen marks, notes, and exclamation marks. They
didn't put a single mark on any other section.

It speaks to large numbers. If you want to talk to large numbers
of people, the only way to do it is through the mass media.

It rallies the troops. Media attention adds momentum to a grassroots initiative. David Engwicht, author of *Reclaiming Our Cities
and Towns,* knows how empowerment can come from media
attention. Group members say, "Did you see we were in the news
again? Isn't it great? We are really starting to get places now."

It makes enemies. According to Herb Gunther of the Public Media Center in San Francisco, "Successful advocacy doesn't make friends. It makes enemies. It points a finger, names names, starts a fight. It tells us who's responsible and how to fight back. It tells us which side we're on."

Getting coverage means risking negative coverage

One of the principal forces marginalizing ordinary people is fear of dealing with the media, which stems from a fear of getting bad press and being misrepresented. Also, many people worry too much about the impact of small errors. Most reporters go out of their way to be kind to citizens involved in public interest actions. Negative press is usually the result of attempts to mislead reporters; of selfish or self-serving actions; or of a group launching attacks on others. Citizens groups face only one real problem: the ineffectiveness of action that gets no media attention.

9.2   Creating Messages

To create your message for the media, start by defining your goals, if you haven't already done so. Invent strategies for reaching your goals, then turn these strategies into messages using the guidelines below. Finally, turn the messages into actual communications products – sound bites, op-eds, e-mail bulletins, and so forth. The sequence looks like this:

goals > strategies > messages> actual communications products

For more on creating strategies see Chapter 7 and Appendix 2.

Message = What people take away

Think of your message as "what" you wish to communicate – what your audience will take away. A good message may generate many different creative communications products or methods to convey the message in actual words and images.

Don't make the mistake of thinking your message is the actual words and images you will use. Consider this message, created by a group of people trying to improve their neighborhood: "East Mount Pleasant has become a desirable place to live." It's a good message, but too dull to work as an effective communications product. It needs creative thinking. For the sake of argument, let's suppose the group steps back and looks at the reputation of East Mount Pleasant. Outsiders believe the neighborhood is unsafe, so if they have a choice, they refuse to move into the area.

The group decides the best strategy is to address the issue of safety. This is a good move for two reasons. First, safety is more a matter of impression than of fact; that is to say, it is more of a media project. Secondly, with this more specific strategy the group can define a more specific message. They decide on: "East Mount Pleasant is safe for kids." This message has more potential for generating convincing communications products. For instance, the group might erect numerous hand-painted wooden cutout signs of kids and balloons on neighborhood streets, with the words "Slow down, children playing" painted on them. The signs would give outsiders the impression the neighborhood was full of kids and probably quite safe.

Create a communications grid

In most cases your messages will have to compete with the messages of your opponents. When there is real opposition, create a communications grid. To do this, you extract messages from what everybody is saying on the issues in dispute and put them into categories: Us on Us, Us on Them, Them on Us, Them on Them.

Let's take an actual example. A large department store in a poor area of town is empty for nine years. Many residents of the area suffered from mental problems and drug addiction. A left-wing provincial government buys the building and promises to turn it into low-income housing. When a right-wing government is elected, it announces it is going to sell the building to a developer. Local residents occupy the derelict building for a week, spending nights sleeping on concrete floors, before they are finally evicted by police. A summary of the views of various opinion leaders produced the following communications grid.

Issue: Using public funds to convert a derelict store into low-income housing

Us on Us	Us on Them	Them on Us	Them on Them
It will revitalize a poor neighborhood	Right-wing politicians only care about cutting taxes for the rich	Providing handouts makes people dependent and reduces the incentive to work	The project is too expensive
People in the area need decent housing	They are breaking a promise to the community		Subsidies distort the housing market
	Government wants to gentrify the area and expel the poor		The private sector should provide housing

---

Taking the time to figure out your opponent's messages makes it much easier to come up with sound bites and other communications that will neutralize an opponent.

Extract your message from what moves your audience

Polling, even informal polling, will help determine what messages resonate with the people you hope to reach. Don't assume your overly involved group is representative of your target audience. Using polling to determine what messages work, and then using these messages, has become standard practice for politicians and advertisers. To maintain a proper balance of interests, civil society needs to adopt similar techniques.

Consider the message an action sends

When an ad hoc citizens group appears on the scene, it is often composed of people with an action agenda. This is fine so long as the agenda helps to achieve the group's objective. Often it does not. Consider a community group that is upset by open drug dealing and street prostitution. The first impulse of many citizens is to go to the press with a collection of horror stories. But this will probably make things worse, reinforcing the idea that the neighborhood is a bad place to live, making it less attractive to families and businesses, and more attractive to drug dealers and pimps.

The characteristics of good messages

Good messages are short and simple. Consider the message "We should discard our old-fashioned first-past-the-post electoral system and replace it with proportional representation or partial proportional representation." It is too long. This would be better: "Our electoral system is out of date."

Good messages motivate. "Take the train today" doesn't motivate. "The train is faster and more relaxing" does.

Good messages are memorable. Noam Chomsky's message that US presidents are international criminals is memorable. His quote: "If we were to apply the standards of the Nuremberg trails today, all post-war US presidents would have to be hanged."

Repeat your message. Your message needs to be repeated or else it will fail to register. One of the main reasons non-profits fail to communicate effectively is that they rarely communicate a message more than once or twice. Cathy Allen stresses repetition in *Taking Back Politics*, her book about running election campaigns.

Her Golden Rule: Get the right message to the right people at least three to five times in the last three weeks of a campaign.

Rooting Out Evil

The message of the Toronto-based peace group Rooting Out Evil is that the US is the greatest threat to world peace; it has large stockpiles of biological, chemical, and nuclear weapons; it refuses to honor or sign international treaties; and it is extremely aggressive. To convey its message the group decided to send a team of arms inspectors to Washington, a version of the United Nations inspectors who were searching for arms in Iraq at the time. This action got wide press coverage because it was novel, topical, and included two newsworthy people, Canadian MP Libby Davies and British MP Alan Simpson.

9.3   Creating Actual Communications

After the creation of messages comes the creation of actual communications products. This might involve converting key messages into a collection of speaking points for your spokesperson. It might involve finding or creating a collection of quotes for use in newspaper and magazine articles. Or it might involve devising actions that illustrate your message or provoke your opponents to make your case for you.

To move from messages to actual communications products you must consider various questions, the most important of which are: who is your intended audience, and how do you make your message newsworthy.

For whom?

To identify your intended audience you should spend some time thinking about who can help you resolve your issue and who stands in the way. It makes no sense to define a communicative action without a clear idea of whom you wish to influence. Is it the general public? Local government? A state or provincial government? A political party? A political leader? A board of trade? A newspaper editorial board? A corporate CEO? The neighbors of a corporate CEO? The buyers of a corporation's products? Foreign consumers? Shareholders? Once you identify your audience you can tailor communications products to fit audience members' interests and their knowledge of an issue.

Is it newsworthy?

Often the best action is media advocacy that presses government to make positive policy changes. In simple terms this amounts to using the media to put the screws on government. Because buying advertising is expensive, non-profits usually try to earn free media coverage. The first step is figuring out how to convert your probably unnewsworthy objectives into newsworthy actions that the media will cover for free.

One of the great difficulties for citizens groups and small non-profits is understanding what makes something newsworthy. The best test is to write the headline for a perfect news piece on your issue – then ask yourself candidly if the news source would actually run such a piece. And would your mom read it?

Newsworthy is:

- Novel
- Emotional
- Shocking, sexy, scandalous
- Humorous, ironic
- Linked to breaking news or a topical news theme
- Simple
- Packaged in an interesting way
- Focused outdoors
- Populated by celebrities or public figures
- About kids or animals
- Likely to include interesting props or bright images
- Of local interest
- Action oriented
- Responsible for arrests
- Something someone is trying to hide

Dramatize your issue to make the news

With a little inventiveness, dull messages can be transformed into newsworthy communications products. This is where citizens groups can have fun. Many books, such as Michael Levine's *Guerrilla PR*, focus on how to create media events of interest to reporters. Stunts that are relevant and photogenic stand a much better chance of receiving TV coverage.

In *Green Fire*, Ian Cohen describes how he dramatized the problem of radioactive tailings remaining as the residue of beach sandmining in his home town of Byron Bay, Australia:

> *In protest against [radioactive residues left behind from sandmining] I formed the Byron Radiation Information Centre – yours truly with a Geiger counter. Greg Tollis and myself plotted the many areas of radiation in the town. Sites included the hospital, a school, an old people's home and private residences. I was not the first to raise the alarm, but I recklessly promoted it in the local media.*
>
> *My most notable venture into journalistic hyperbole followed the discovery of radiation under the local girl guide's hall; the press release was entitled "Brownies Fry."*
>
> *My truck became a rolling billboard. On the front doors were large radiation symbols with the caption "Byron Shire resident – radioactive." I regularly parked my vehicle outside local real estate offices. Government action was soon forthcoming. . .*

The same story isn't news

Once the media have covered a story, they aren't likely to cover it again unless some new development makes it news again.

They may produce an update if some time has gone by with no coverage and the issue is still relevant. They may cover an old story with a new focus such as an anniversary, a breakthrough, an event involving a celebrity, a new controversy, an uncovered injustice, a local interest, a milestone, a human interest story, or a seasonal story. They might also return to an old story if you can link it to what is happening at the moment. The best person to contact is the reporter who last covered the story.

Aim for an unfolding story

Events that unfold over time are the best events for media coverage because they can generate a series of stories over a long period. When the RCMP attacked people protesting an APEC conference in Vancouver, the RCMP Public Complaints Commission was convened to hold an inquiry. Protesters, viewing the inquiry as a whitewash, almost made the tactical mistake of walking out. The inquiry generated a huge volume of additional press and gave the protesters a public platform for the next two years.

9.4   Media Relations

Building relationships with key reporters will make it much easier to be effective in the media. Particularly important are working relationships with reporters who write stories in your area of interest. Take the following steps to improve your media relations.

Keep track of who's doing what. Keep an up-to-date media list of reporters and producers with names and contact information – phone, fax, and e-mail. Ask them about deadlines so you can avoid calling when they are busy. In Canada, *Matthews Media Directory* lists the key people in every newspaper, radio, and TV station with direct-line phone numbers. The directory is continually updated and is expensive, but you can find it at most large public libraries.

Build your credibility. Aim for absolute accuracy. The worst thing you can do is embarrass reporters by giving them bad information. Make sure your information is accurate. It you're not sure, ask the journalist for his/her deadline, then call back with the facts. Don't exaggerate your case. Help the journalist sort out an issue by representing the views of your adversaries accurately.

Limit the number of goofy stunts. If your spokesperson always wears a dinosaur suit, reporters are less likely to treat you seriously. If you want to include dinosaurs, partner with performance art activists – they can provide the spectacle while you provide the facts.

Increase your public visibility. The more you are quoted on an issue, the more reporters will see you as an authority. Assume *every* chat with a reporter is on the record.

Help reporters do their job. Because reporters are always in a rush, they are far more likely to call you if you:
- return phone calls promptly,
- know your issue,
- have hard facts at your fingertips,
- have quotable quotes ready to go,
- have useful phone numbers at your fingertips, and
- help them find additional information fast. Call back every time, even if all you can say is, "We're working to get that information for you."

Reporters like people who make their work easy.

Pitch story ideas. One of the best ways to get attention is to pitch story ideas to reporters, columnists, and TV or radio producers. Get into the habit of thinking up good story ideas. When you think you've got one, pitch it to a reporter who has written articles about your issue. Your pitch should last no longer than a minute, be framed to your advantage, and refer to visuals if you're aiming at TV.

Pitch personal, then reframe. The media like stories about people, so pitch stories with strong personal, emotional, or human interest content. Once you get a bite, try to frame the story so it becomes an illustration of the need for the changes you advocate – in other words, try to establish a mobilizing frame. For more on mobilizing frames see Appendix 3.

Find media professionals who will help. Seek help from the people in your community who work for newspapers, radio, and television stations. They can provide advice on what is newsworthy, how to get attention, and who to call. Most will not want to be visibly involved, but in the background they will be invaluable.

If a story has errors. Many groups fret needlessly over small errors in stories. Small errors are normal. If your message comes through, they usually don't matter. If a story has serious factual errors that alter how people will view an issue, call the reporter. Retractions are usually a waste of time, but a responsible beat reporter will try to get it right next time.

9.5 Timing

Your action has a better chance of getting covered if it is adjusted so it connects to a "news hook" – an event that is news or is about to become news. Canadian students protesting the Chinese occupation of Tibet usually get little media attention, but they received a lot of coverage when they staged their protest at the airport just as the prime minister was leaving on a trade mission to China.

Buy-Nothing-Day invisible on a nothing day

Adbusters magazine promoted its Buy-Nothing-Day for a long time with little coverage until it changed the date to the biggest shopping day of the year in the US, the day after Thanksgiving. Media that cover the shopping binge as part of their "editorial calendar" inevitably mention *Adbusters* and Buy-Nothing-Day.

Be ready to link to upcoming news

You can prepare press releases, sound bites, and visual stunts for events that you know are coming up. The best bets for coverage are linking to hard news stories where your group is the only one seeking attention, but you can also link to predictable soft news occasions: back to school; Valentine's Day; Remembrance Day; fashion shows; International Women's Day; yearly festivals, races, tournaments.

Link to anticipated news

- a court decision,
- the tabling of a bill,
- a visit by a national politician,
- a visit by a foreign dignitary,
- the arrival of a big ship,
- an international conference,
- the release of a report,
- the anniversary of an historic event, or
- an election.

React quickly to breaking news

Opportunities to access the media increase dramatically if you can respond to breaking news within a day. This requires an organizational structure that permits rapid response. Frontline workers must be able to respond without the approval of a board or a committee of overseers.

It is a good idea to create an Issue Response Plan that lists the steps to take if an issue arises that requires immediate response. It should include a media phone list; the phone numbers of suitable spokespersons and alternates if they cannot be reached; plus the phone numbers of people who must be contacted before a response is made, and their alternates.

Best times, best days, best seasons

If there is no useful breaking news, consider making news with your own event. Try to time the event so that it occurs between 10 am and 3 pm, Monday to Thursday. As a rule, avoid ratings weeks and Fridays. Governments often release bad news on Fridays, hoping it will get less attention because reporters have left early.

There are many exceptions. Sunday can be a good day because often little is happening locally, but TV newscasts still must generate stories and papers must generate a Monday paper. Sunday is also a day when more citizens can take part in an event. The problem with Sunday is that most news outlets are down to a skeleton staff, so they may not have a reporter available to cover your event. If this happens, phone the assignment desk with an offer of interviews and pictures.

The week before and the week after Christmas can be good periods, especially if you can invent a way to link your issue to Christmas. Christmas is the season when huge numbers of bored people watch TV endlessly and read and reread newspapers, so getting coverage at this time can be a huge advantage.

July and August can also be good months. With a lot of reporters on holiday, many news organizations welcome anything that will easily fill up space or time. The disadvantage of summers, Sundays, and Christmas is the story may end up in the hands of a junior reporter or intern, or be ignored because of the lack of any kind of reporter.

9.6   Surveys, Petitions, Research

Surveys and polls

Because the media love surveys and polls, you can usually count on getting a story based on the results. Best of all, you can set up the survey or poll to frame content in a way that suits your message. A complete how-to on conducting polls and surveys requires a book of its own, but this section provides a quick look at simple surveys undertaken as a way of getting media attention.

Omnibus polls. Most polling companies do omnibus telephone polls on a regular schedule to accommodate clients who cannot afford a complete custom poll of their own. With this kind of poll, your questions are combined with questions from other clients. If you can boil down what you want to ask to a few questions, you can get a newsworthy result for hundreds of dollars rather than thousands.

Burger polls. If you want accurate data, you need to use a credible polling company. Quick surveys make no pretense at accuracy. Nevertheless, they can make the news as snapshots or samples of public opinion. The hamburger poll is an example of a quick survey. Burger joints offer exactly the same burger under two different names, such as the GoreBurger and the BushBurger. Then they tally the sales of each.

There are all sorts of ways of modifying the restaurant poll. For instance, a group could arrange to print issue sheets as place mats. Waiters could then offer a variety of bills related to positions on the issue and ask people what kind of bill they would like to receive.

Sidewalk surveys. Sidewalk surveys are usually conducted by the media – frequently by radio and TV reporters. If you have an idea for a sidewalk survey, you might consider pitching it to a producer. Most sidewalk surveys ask passersby to answer one simple question, or to make one simple choice.

Documentary surveys. The graphic results of a videotaped survey provide great content for a video news release or a video documentary. The CBC TV program *This Hour Has 22 Minutes* got some good footage when it videotaped a survey of Harvard business students. Initial questions showed that students believed Harvard was the top business school in the land. A second set of questions showed they knew next to nothing about elementary world affairs.

Michael Moore's short-lived *TV Nation* pushed the idea of a video survey even further. One piece was about how cab drivers routinely ignore blacks. *TV Nation* videotaped cab drivers repeatedly driving by a black man, only to stop to pick up a white person just past him. Cab drivers claimed not to have seen the black man, but adding a succession of increasingly larger signs with flashing lights and giant arrows failed to make any difference.

Ambush surveys. With an ambush survey you set up an opportunity for a targeted group of people to do something illegal, embarrassing, or revealing. You then secretly record the result and turn it over to the media.

Alan Borovoy, head of the Canadian Civil Liberties Association, recommends this kind of survey as a way of accessing the media. In his book *Uncivil Obedience*, he describes how in the 1960s he set up an ambush survey to expose job discrimination by government. He had people posing as employers seeking staff call 21 federal employment offices. They asked if federal officials would screen out certain minority applicants. Incredibly, 17 of the 21 offices agreed. Borovoy announced the results of the survey to a live audience at a human rights conference. It became the lead item on the CBC national news.

Petitions

Petitions are the most common form of citizen survey, but they are far from the most effective. Typically they use up a great deal of grassroots energy, while achieving very little. There are some exceptions. A petition that indicates local feelings on an uncontentious issue will often sway local government especially if there are no cost or legal implications. A petition that is long enough to be rolled out like a red carpet or tied around a building can become a central element of a media event. A petition process can also be a simple way of informing a small number of people about an issue.

Original research

The results of original research can garner media attention and spur government action. When the Canadian Physicians for the Environment became alarmed at injuries involving jet skis, they decided to carry out a study. The results of the study and subsequent media interviews led to legislation requiring training and licensing for jet ski users.

Access to information requests

To create the impression of openness, many governments have passed "access to information" or "freedom of information" legislation that permits public access to information held by government. This is important because governments usually try to hide scandals, screw-ups, and information that would force them to address an issue they would rather ignore.

Various on-line sources will tell you how to write a freedom of information request. Your request can't be a trawling expedition; it has to be specific. One way to make it specific is to have a friendly government insider tell you what to ask for. Another way is to focus on any involvement of a public body with a private entity. Yet another way is to limit your request to a narrow window of time. There is usually no limit on the number of requests you can make, so when in doubt, make a lot.

Sometimes access to information slows to a snail's pace when the information you request is really embarrassing. If this happens, the best route is to ask your friendly government insider to leak the embarrassing material to you.

Because the media is immediately interested in anything government wants to keep hidden, access to information requests often lead to front-page stories.

9.7 Media Advisories/News Releases

A media advisory is sent out before an event, a news release is sent out during or immediately after.

Media advisories

Send out a media advisory one or two days in advance when you wish to alert the media to an imminent newsworthy event. Media advisories are often structured as teasers, providing enough information to get reporters out to the event without giving away the whole story. Don't make the mistake of thinking this is all you have to do to get the attention of reporters. A media advisory needs to be part of a much larger effort that includes phoning reporters and pitching story ideas.

If you are concerned an action may not come off, skip the media advisory and phone in a tip after the action begins.

News releases

Write a news release on your group's letterhead and issue it during or immediately after a newsworthy event. Follow the accepted format. At the top left, in normal type, put: For immediate release, and the date. Next, create a strong newspaper-style headline that will interest an editor who has to shuffle through hundreds of news releases every day. The first sentence of the copy should contain the most important fact in your story. It should also explain the headline. The rest of the release should cover the essentials of who, what, where, when, and why. Break the copy into short paragraphs of one or two sentences. Keep the whole thing to one page. Type <30> in the center of the page at the end of the release; if you need to go to a second page, center <MORE> at the bottom of the first page. At the very end, after <30>, add a final line: Contact: (name and phone number).

Make it grab. Rewrite the headline and first sentence until they have enough grab. If you saw them in a newspaper, would the headline and first sentence make you want to read the article? Organize the rest of the release in an inverted pyramid style, with the strongest material first and the least important last. Test the release by reading it out loud to someone who is not as close to the issue as you are.

Consider a backgrounder. If you need to help reporters make sense of something complicated, add two to three additional pages with the heading "Backgrounder."

Offer photos and documents. If you have good photos, documents, or published backup material, offer them in the news release. Be prepared to send digital photos by e-mail if you get a request.

Phone releases, reminders. Faxing a release without any personal contact is usually a waste of time. It's easy for a news organization to ignore a piece of paper, but not so easy to ignore a phone call. For big events, fax your news release to a specific reporter, then follow up with a phone call. For simple actions, consider phoning in the story without a release.

Take steps to avoid immediate disposal. With so many groups and businesses faxing out large numbers of news releases, most media organizations receive huge numbers of faxes every day. To make sure your release gets noticed, send it to the attention of an actual reporter or producer, and follow it up with a phone call.

Alternatively, pay an organization like Canada Newswire or PR Newswire in the US to send your release out over the wire. Releases received by wire are less likely to be discarded because they arrive the same way as regular news. Either way, you still need to follow up with a phone call.

E-mail news releases. You can also send your news release directly to reporters by e-mail. To make sure it is opened, take time to create a good headline for the subject of the e-mail, or better, talk to the reporter before it goes out. Follow the usual press release guidelines for the body of the e-mail.

If you have photos available, you might use html e-mail, which can embed jpeg images. Avoid attachments; most news organizations trash unsolicited e-mail with attachments to avoid viruses.

9.8   Newspaper Editorial Pages

Op-eds

Op-eds are longer opinion pieces placed opposite the newspaper's editorial page. This outlet is often overlooked by activists, but it is a great way to get your story out.

Begin by phoning the op-ed page editor and pitching what you want to write. He or she will usually respond by suggesting some adjustments to content and direction. This should be enough to get started. You won't get a commitment to publish until the editor sees your finished copy.

> **When writing an op-ed, keep these tips in mind:**
>
> Submit between 600 and 800 words.
>
> Write active paragraphs containing two to three sentences each.
>
> Set up the op-ed as a controversial polemic – an argument that challenges mainstream views. David Beers, a former editor at Mother Jones, suggests the following structure:
>
> 1. Headline
> 2. Thesis
> 3. Bulleted support for the thesis
> 4. Anticipated objections from readers, plus your responses
> 5. Restatement of the thesis
> 6. Finally, a call to action that spells out what politicians or the public should do
>
> You might also suggest or provide photos.

If the issue is of broad significance, consider submitting your op-ed piece to different papers in different places. If you are trying to influence a particular target audience, send it to the paper they read. If your audience is federal politicians, that means you will send it to a paper in Ottawa or Washington.

Submit the op-ed when it connects to what is happening. Other good times are just before holidays and during the summer.

Editorial board meetings

Arranging a meeting with the editorial board of a large newspaper will often fix a screwy media perspective and sometimes generate a favorable editorial. Most large city papers will have a couple of editorial board meetings per week. Call the paper and ask to speak to the person who sets these up. Offer a one-page brief on why you want to talk to the board and what you will cover. It is a good idea to try to set up an editorial board meeting when a special guest comes to town.

Letters to the editor

Common Cause did a study that showed letters to the editor were the most effective way to influence politicians. When written by someone who is good with words, a letter to the editor can take little time to produce, but have a big impact. Surveys consistently show that letters to the editor receive very high readership.

Tips for writing letters to the editor:

- Send letters to small community newspapers; they receive fewer and are more likely to print yours.

- Limit the letter to 100 words. Shorter letters are more likely to get read and less likely to get edited.

- Consider a clever one- or two-line letter. They always get read.

- Consider responding to a previous letter or to a recent column.

- Use mild ridicule if you want to unhinge a politician.

- Use active verbs, concrete nouns, short sentences, and short paragraphs.

- Fax or e-mail your piece directly to the letters editor.

- Letters to the editor are considered opinion. If they contain facts that require checking, they may not get printed. If your facts are really important, cite the source at the bottom of the page so they can be checked.

- If your letters never get printed, call and ask why.

9.9   Video News Releases

A video news release or VNR is the single most effective way of getting your message to a mass audience. A VNR is a short video piece about your issue, made to look as if it were produced by a TV news crew. High-quality copies of VNRs are distributed to TV stations in a broadcast format such as Beta SP.

Most TV stations claim they don't use VNRs. However, most do if the footage is good.

A professional two-minute VNR used to cost between $5,000 and $15,000, too much for most small groups. But high quality video production is now something you can do yourself. Inexpensive digital video (DV) cameras and desktop video editing software like Apple's IMovie and Final Cut have dramatically reduced equipment and editing costs.

To produce a good VNR requires someone with enough experience to be able to shoot and edit the footage so that it looks like news. Try to find a freelancer with experience shooting video for a TV station.

When creating a VNR, keep the following in mind:

—Make it objective. Begin and end with material that supports your position. In the middle you might include people who oppose your position; it will make the piece seem more objective, more like news.

—Consider shooting actions at remote locations that are too expensive for regular news crews to access. Shoot any important event the press might not attend.

—Shoot b-roll (background roll) of any visually interesting event you undertake for later use in VNRs, public service announcements, and video documentaries. Supplement an edited VNR with b-roll snippets so that TV stations can customize your VNR.

—Consider shooting a VNR before an announcement or press conference. Ideally this will consist of a coherent, edited, two- to three-minute piece followed by b-roll snippets separated by black. Label your VNR with a short description of each chunk, with timecode start and end times. Greenpeace has been very successful getting its message out by providing visually interesting videotape in this format.

—Consider stock houses and video libraries to uncover additional background footage. Also look for documentaries on your issue; some producers may allow you to use parts of their work.

9.10   Press Conferences

A press conference is usually the wrong way to attract attention. Media often don't show up, particularly if the press conference focuses on a community issue. They will show up if you have celebrities, important people, a hot issue, or you promise to deliver newsworthy information.

Before the press conference

Precede a news conference with a faxed or e-mailed news advisory that hints at what will be revealed without giving the story away. Print media kits that contain the press release, brief biographies of speakers, and a two- to three-page backgrounder summarizing history, salient facts, quotes, and other contextual information that might be useful to a reporter. Consider including a couple of recent articles on your issue and summaries of credible reports or studies. Keep press kits thin. Hand them out to reporters in exchange for a business card or their name on a sign-in sheet.

Location, time, setup

For TV, choose an interesting visual setting that's appropriate to the story. An exterior location is best, but have an indoor backup in case of bad weather. It's also better to have a venue that is too small rather than one that is too big. The setting should be close to media outlets so reporters and crews don't have far to travel. Hold the press conference between 10 & 11 am or 1:30 & 3 pm.

Place a typeset sign identifying your organization in front of your speaker, ideally just below the face, where cameras will catch it. Provide a space in front of your speakers where camera operators can set up tripods and run microphone cables.

The press conference

Invite your supporters to attend. It will create a buzz and the feeling that your issue matters to lots of people.

Use props. Provide speakers with props that make good pictures – a giant check to show uncollected corporate taxes, an extended drift net to emphasize the threat of uncontrolled fisheries, a cross-section of a huge tree to show what is being cut down. Props also help at community meetings. At one meeting in Vancouver, a woman spoke about the problem of street prostitution while holding her four-year-old daughter in one arm and a sack of dirty needles and condoms in the other.

Limit the number of speakers, and the length of speeches. Limit the number of speakers to three, and their speaking time to five minutes max. Allow ten minutes for questions. A moderator should limit speaking time and deal with questions. Place the name of your group in front of each speaker.

Prepare for poor attendance. For media that fail to show up, issue a news release describing the event, complete with quotes and an offer of high quality jpeg images. Phone key reporters who did attend with offers of one-to-one interviews. For e-mailed news releases, consider including a complete web address that editors can click to review digital photos of the event.

Use your opponent's press conference

The media find press conferences dull because they usually provide a single point of view and very little conflict. You can improve your opponent's news conference by adding the conflict it lacks. If your opponent is a politician, even better. You can improve public debate by providing another point of view.

Ask a contact in the media to let you know in advance about scheduled press conferences. Attend the press conference and find a position close to the front where TV cameras will include both you and your opponent in the same shot. Then proceed to ask a barrage of forceful questions. Don't allow brush-offs or attempts to switch to milder questions. Make sure you come well armed with facts so you don't appear to be a wing nut.

9.11   Ads That Become News

For groups with little money, paid advertising is usually out of the question. Money for a few ads or billboards is often wasted because advertising, to be effective, requires a lot of repetition in many different places. But there is one opportunity for a tiny ad budget to make a difference, and that is with a controversial ad that becomes newsworthy. When an ad becomes news it gets the repetition and exposure it needs to make an impact.

The animal rights group People for the Ethical Treatment of Animals (PETA) has been very successful creating ads that become news. It does this by creating ads that offend some person or group, which then cries foul. If print media pick up the story, they can get a high quality print version of the ad directly from PETA's web site, www.peta.org.

9.12   Cable TV Production

Public access cable TV provides a forum where groups can air interviews and features on their particular issues. Cable licensing often requires the cable operator to provide airtime for "community" productions. If your message has a radical or anti-corporate flavor, this may be one of the few places you can be heard.

If you don't know video. Many cable operators will provide audio and video equipment, as well as train people to operate it. You can also join a video cooperative to get training and equipment. Some local cable stations will produce video on your behalf using in-house staff. Call the cable station to find out how access works.

Consider forming a video production group. Rather than using the station's resources or doing it yourself, try to find someone with training in video production. You may be able to form an ad hoc production team around this person, with people assigned the various roles of camera/sound operator, microphone boom operator, writer, lighting technician and interviewer or director. The person with training can show others what to do. Switching roles will keep everyone interested.

Shoot digital. Technical advances have made it possible to shoot broadcast-quality digital video on inexpensive cameras, then edit raw footage using inexpensive software on a desktop computer. These advances mean that citizens groups with small budgets can produce high-quality video. Until the conversion to digital is complete, TV stations will expect you to dub digital mini-DV tape to Beta SP for broadcast.

Look for extra mileage. You may be able get extra mileage by re-editing and repackaging a finished video. Many cable stations will air good documentaries assembled from a collection of shorter news productions. They will also repeatedly air a one-minute public service announcements (psa). Sometimes you can easily make a psa by cutting bits from an exiting documentary and adding a new voice-over. Schools, libraries, museums, stock houses, documentary producers, courseware producers, conference organizers, and organizations offering video over the web may also be interested in video re-edited for their audiences.

9.13   Radio

Public broadcasters such as CBC and NPR air daily radio shows that include a mix of news, entertainment, interviews, and discussion. One of the best ways to advance an issue is to bring an expert into town, then arrange to get this person onto one of these radio shows. Particularly effective is the person who has already accomplished somewhere else what you have proposed locally. In addition to media appearances, try to schedule meetings and lunches with key politicians, business groups, and bureaucrats. Offer a free evening public lecture as well – it makes a good conclusion to a radio interview.

If your group can get a spokesperson on a live radio show, you can actually shape the news because you won't be edited as you would be on TV or in print. To sound good, write down short chunks of commentary that convey your message; and take them with you to the interview. You can also offer an interview by cell phone from a location where something is happening. Radio reporters like to do interviews with "actuals" – background sounds that provide texture, immediacy, and the feeling of being there.

News sound bites

Good sound bites are particularly useful to radio reporters. But they are hard to create on the spot. If a reporter calls and asks for an interview, ask about the story angle, but don't respond right away. Say you will call right back. It will give you time to think about your response, and prepare a collection of appetizing sound bites.

Consider talk radio

Because most activists don't listen to commercial talk radio, they often ignore its potential. The listeners of talk radio are numerous, interested in politics, and may be the right audience if you want to move beyond preaching to the converted. Listen to as much talk radio as you can to identify a program that might be interested in your topic. Next, call the producer of the show to pitch the topic and the guest. If you're invited on as a guest, take the following steps to prepare for your appearance.

- Familiarize yourself with the host and the program format.
- Practice vocal inflection and the avoidance of *ah* and *um*.
- Ask your supporters to call, and get someone to tape the show.
- Warm up your voice. Just before going on, take a deep breath.
- Mention your group's name and phone number.
- Bring some notes for reference, but don't read your responses.
- Choose a studio interview over a phone interview.
- Use humor to stay afloat with a hostile host.
- Smile on radio; people will be able to hear it.
- If you have some great tape, bring it along and have it played.
- Practice bridging, described below.

9.14 Preparing for Interviews

If you, your group, or your issue appears in the morning paper, you may get a call from a radio or TV station. If you don't get a call, it's an opportunity to call them. In either case, you need to know how to handle an interview.

Find the right spokesperson

To avoid muddles and embarrassment it's best to choose one person from your group to act as spokesperson. Because the largest part of communication is non-verbal, this person should give off the right non-verbal information. Your spokesperson should look and sound relaxed, friendly, cooperative, and trustworthy. He or she should also display a sense of humor. Studies of persuasion conclude that convincing spokespersons are those people that we view as being like ourselves. For most audiences this means someone who can create the impression of urgency without panic, and concern without anger; someone who can be critical but not nasty, intelligent but not arrogant, progressive but not radical.

Prepare for TV interviews

Besides compelling visuals, TV and news radio require a compressed way of talking. You can prepare for this by turning your message into a collection of five or six sound bites, about 5 to 15 seconds long, that convey your message in a forceful manner. Sound bites are most effective when they use active verbs and concrete nouns. "The prime minister shuts his eyes to human rights abuse whenever it's good for business." "Stop making deals with China until China stops sterilizing Tibetan women."

Questions can make great sound bites and put your adversary on the spot: "How much was the governor paid by the health insurance lobby to kill this proposal for universal healthcare?" "Should the richest country in the world slam the door on poor people who get sick?" "What's more important: our health or private health care profits?"

What's really matters on TV

A UCLA study revealed that:

- what you say accounts for 7 percent of what is believed,
- how you say it accounts for 38 percent of what is believed,
- how you look accounts for 55 percent of what is believed.

Tailor sound bites

You can improve sound bites by adding the following elements:

Local relevance: "Our city hall hired the PR firm that engineered the cover-up of Chinese government atrocities in Tibet."

Uniqueness: "For the first time in Canadian history the prime minister has recognized Tibet with an official visit."

Immediacy: "We just learned that Chinese authorities plan to blow up another Buddhist monastery in Tibet."

Do's and don'ts for TV appearances:

- Dress in classic clothing.

- Consider bringing along interesting visual props.

- Smile. It's the best way to bring people to your side.

- Smile when handed a tough question; then move to your message.

- Look at the interviewer, not the camera.

- Take a deep breath before you speak in order to relax.

- Stand up straight, and don't fidget

- If you stumble, stop, apologize, and start over. Stumbles can be eliminated during editing.

Practice often helps a lot. Ideally, record practice sessions with a video camera with someone acting as a difficult interviewer. How do you come across? If you are a natural, practicing your delivery may make you seem stiff and artificial, but most people can use some practice. If you decide you need practice:

- Aim for the right nonverbal flavor.

- Practice delivering your message in as few words as possible.

- Practice speaking slowly.

- Practice body language. For example practice raising and lowering your voice and/or your eyebrows for emphasis. You might also practice hand gestures. .

Bridging over tricky questions

People who are not used to live interviews try to answer all questions directly. This is not a good idea because it lets the interviewer control the show. Instead, you should use the interview to get across your messages. Most media training gives people a lot of practice responding to difficult or irrelevant questions with a bridge or segue to statements that get across key messages. Here are some examples of bridges:

Big Picture

Interpret tough questions broadly, then bridge to your message.

Q If we reduced consumption, wouldn't it ruin the economy?

A We've become fixated on economic growth. We need to start asking what the economy is for. . .

Brush-off

Say you don't know the answer, then switch to your message.

Q How much money do unions contribute to your campaign?

A I don't have those figures at hand. What I can say is. .

Brief answer brush-off

Acknowledge the difficult question, then veer to your message.

Q How many jobs will be lost if we turn this area into a park?

A Very few considering the size of the area. The thing to remember is that the park will benefit everyone.

Highlight

The point to remember is. . .

Refocus

A better question is. . .

I sure the public would also want to know. . .

Here is a more sensible way to look at the issue. . .

Another approach is. . .

Let me clarify something. . .

There is another way of looking at that. . .

However. . .

Small concession

It is also true that. . .

That may be true, but it is not the whole story. . .

Selective response

The most important point you raise is. . .

9.15 Narrowcasting

Small advocacy groups can create progressive change by sending a steady stream of material to a relatively small number of people who have the power to bring about change. These include politicians, senior bureaucrats, producers, editors, reporters, and other opinion leaders.

Infective microfaxing

Infective microfaxing is based on two simple ideas. First, people always read anything that is half a page or less. Second, they absorb information and values from what they read over and over.

Infective microfaxing requires sending out weekly faxes of published articles to key bureaucrats, leaders, journalists, and politicians. These faxes are tear-outs from published material – news items, summary articles, book reviews, conclusions of studies or polls – no longer than half a page. Suitable pieces often come from the front and end matter in journals and magazines.

Infective microfaxes work like a charm. Recipients who receive a steady stream of objective print material with the same message will gradually incorporate it into the way they see the world. The only downside of microfaxing is that it takes a regular commitment of time to do it well.

An e-mail news service

Microfaxing really amounts to getting your message out by providing a fax clipping service. Another possibility is to provide influential people with an e-mail clipping service. Target less-visible assistants, advisors, consultants, and deputies. These people actually read their e-mail, whereas busy politicians often don't.

Expand your list through a regular routine – if you send out material on Thursday, you might try to add five new names every Thursday.

Provide a summary of news related to your issue. Each item should contain a reference to a source and, if possible, a link to a website with the full article, a longer version, or supporting images or graphs. Links can also connect to additional material on your own website. The broader the coverage and the wider the range of views, the more it will be read and trusted.

C H A P T E R

Confrontation 101

10.1 Hold On

If you picked up this book and immediately flipped to this section, you are probably on the wrong track. Confrontation is generally not the best strategy for citizens who want to effect positive change. Confrontational tactics can be counterproductive and undermine the larger project of increasing citizen involvement because they make opponents dig in, they wear citizens out, and they leave everyone feeling miserable. If you have a problem you are trying to address, turn back to the sections on community organizing, strategic thinking, and media advocacy.

It is important to recognize that smart activists try to avoid confrontational tactics even in confrontational situations. A good example is Mahatma Gandhi.

Gandhi's top eight methods for converting an opponent

Gandhi suggested these methods to convert opponents who control you or your group. Conversion refers to the process by which an opponent comes around to embrace your objectives.

1. Refrain from violence and hostility.

2. Refrain from humiliating an opponent.

3. Maintain contact with an opponent. This is absolutely necessary if conversion is to succeed.

4. Develop empathy, good will, and patience toward an opponent.

5. Attempt to obtain your opponent's trust by:
   - being truthful,
   - being open about your intentions,
   - using chivalry (for example, being kind if the other side experiences an unrelated difficulty), and
   - making behavior inoffensive without compromising the issue at hand.
6. Demonstrate trust in an opponent.
7. Make visible sacrifices for one's cause. Here it is best if the suffering of the aggrieved is made visible.
8. Carry on constructive work. Address parts of the problem you can address. Make improvements where you can. Participate in activities that all people see as contributing to everyone's common welfare.

This is the best you can do. If you fail to convert an opponent it may be due to external factors beyond your control.

10.2 Rules for Radicals

In 1971, Saul Alinsky wrote an entertaining classic on grassroots organizing titled *Rules for Radicals*. Those who prefer cooperative tactics describe the book as out-of-date. Nevertheless, it provides some of the best advice on confrontational tactics. Alinsky begins this way:

> *What follows is for those who want to change the world from what it is to what they believe it should be. The Prince was written by Machiavelli for the Haves on how to hold power. Rules for Radicals is written for the Have-Nots on how to take it away.*

His "rules" derive from many successful campaigns where he helped poor people fight power and privilege.

For Alinsky, organizing is the process of highlighting what is wrong and convincing people they can actually do something about it. The two are linked. If people feel they don't have the power to change a bad situation, they stop thinking about it.

According to Alinsky, the organizer – especially a paid organizer from outside – must first overcome suspicion and establish credibility. Next the organizer must begin the task of agitating: rubbing resentments, fanning hostilities, and searching out controversy. As well, the organizer must attack apathy and prevailing patterns of community life to get people to participate. Alinsky would say, "The first step in community organization is a community disorganization."

Through a process combining hope and resentment, the organizer tries to create a "mass army" that brings in as many recruits as possible from local organizations, churches, services groups, labor unions, corner gangs, and individuals.

Alinsky provides a collection of rules to guide the process. But he emphasizes these rules must be translated into real-life tactics that are fluid and responsive to the situation at hand.

Rules for Radicals

Rule 1 Power is not only what you have, but what an opponent thinks you have. If your organization is small, hide your numbers in the dark and raise a din that will make everyone think you have many more people than you do.

Rule 2 Never go outside the experience of your people. The result is confusion, fear, and retreat.

Rule 3 Whenever possible, go outside the experience of an opponent. Here you want to cause confusion, fear, and retreat.

Rule 4 Make opponents live up to their own book of rules. "You can kill them with this, for they can no more obey their own rules than the Christian church can live up to Christianity."

Rule 5 Ridicule is man's most potent weapon. It's hard to counterattack ridicule, and it infuriates the opposition, which then reacts to your advantage.

Rule 6 A good tactic is one your people enjoy. "If your people aren't having a ball doing it, there is something very wrong with the tactic."

Rule 7 A tactic that drags on for too long becomes a drag. Commitment may become ritualistic as people turn to other issues.

Rule 8 Keep the pressure on. Use different tactics and actions and use all events of the period for your purpose. "The major premise for tactics is the development of operations that will maintain a constant pressure upon the opposition. It is this that will cause the opposition to react to your advantage."

Rule 9 The threat is more terrifying than the thing itself. When Alinsky leaked word that large numbers of poor people were going to tie up the washrooms of O'Hare Airport, Chicago city authorities quickly agreed to act on a longstanding commitment to a ghetto organization. They imagined the mayhem as thousands of passengers poured off airplanes to discover every washroom occupied. Then they imagined the international embarrassment and the damage to the city's reputation.

Rule 10 The price of a successful attack is a constructive alternative. Avoid being trapped by an opponent or an interviewer who says, "Okay, what would you do?"

Rule 11 Pick the target, freeze it, personalize it, polarize it. Don't try to attack abstract corporations or bureaucracies. Identify a responsible individual. Ignore attempts to shift or spread the blame.

According to Alinsky, the main job of the organizer is to bait an opponent into reacting. "The enemy properly goaded and guided in his reaction will be your major strength."

Sometimes your enemy does not react in a helpful way. When protesters showed up at the Trident nuclear submarine base in Bangor, Washington, the authorities invited them in and fed them sandwiches. In doing so they defused opposition to the largest buildup of nuclear weapons on the planet. Newspaper photos of people munching sandwiches made the protest look like a picnic.

10.3 Citizen Investigations

One way citizens groups can wield great power is by exposing lies, conflicts of interest, failures to enforce the law, misspent public funds, and incompetent behavior. Conducting an in-depth investigation is a tactic that should be part of an overall strategy. When something is uncovered, you need to exploit it in a way that leads to movement toward your objective.

Some of the most revealing information is uncovered through freedom of information requests. For details, see 9.6 "Access to information requests." For suggestions on conducting investigations in the US, consult the third edition of *Organizing for Social Change: The Midwest Academy Manual for Activists* by Kim Bobo, Jackie Kendall, and Steve Max. Other useful how-to books are *Get the Facts on Anyone*, third edition, by Dennis King, and the *Reporter's Handbook: An Investigator's Guide to Documents and Techniques* by Steve Weinberg. For help conducting Canadian investigations get a copy of *How to Research Almost Anything* by Stephen Overbury.

Communicating via the web has distinct advantages. The corporate mass media are difficult and expensive to access, and they control the final result. The web is easy to access, especially with web authoring programs like Macromedia's Dreamweaver and Adobe's Golive. It's an inexpensive way to present volumes of text and first-rate color images. And best of all, you have complete control over content.

As good as this sounds, the reality of communicating over the web has not lived up to its promise. Activists have overlooked opportunities presented by the new medium. For the most part they fail to "pull" people to their sites. Lack of pull combined with the vast array of competing material means that activist sites get less attention, and are less effective than they could be.

Pull audiences with information

Unlike regular advertising, which "pushes" messages to audiences, websites have to "pull" audiences by offering something sufficiently attractive that people will visit the site. If you are thinking of putting up an activist site:

- identify who you want to influence,
- figure out what they want, and
- provide a way they can get it on your site.

One way to pull an audience is to provide fast, free, clear information. For activists this usually means providing facts, commentary, and how-to information that mainstream media ignore or distort. A variation is to tailor information and images for students doing school projects. Teachers tell students to use the library for research, but students from grade 3 all the way to college use the web far more often.

Pull audiences with humor

Besides information, people look for entertainment on the web. Ridicule provides good entertainment and is an excellent way to unhinge a target. Begin by messing around with your target's photo. You might show your target dressed as an aristocrat or a pirate, or growing a Pinocchio nose.

Satire and opinion are legitimate forms of expression, but remember to get your facts straight; the web will not protect you from libel.

Increase visiting time with good web design

Follow the rules for web design found in various guides available on the web.

- Make sure the site loads quickly with the most common kind of connection.
- Make sure the site is easy to understand and navigate.
- Make the site attractive and try to make it coherent with common type and layout across different pages.
- Finally, use your imagination. Your website does not have to look like everything else out there.

To make sure everything works, test the site with different versions of different browsers. Ask friends for feedback.

Ways to get people to your site

Most hosts provide web stats that show how many people visit each page and where visitors were before they came to your site. You can use this information to increase traffic to your site.

Other ways to get people to your site

—Put your site address on your business cards, in your e-mail signature, and on letterhead, press releases, and any other information you send out.

—Identify well-executed, friendly sites. Send the webmasters for these sites an e-mail complimenting them on their site. Then ask if they will put up a link to your site. Link exchanges will bring people to your site and improve your rating with many search engines.

—Ask anyone writing an article on your organization or work to include your website address in the article.

—Paid ads, if they are engaging, will bring people to your site. These include billboards, transit ads, signs, bulletin board notices, free postcards, magazine and newspaper ads, magnetic ads for the sides of cars, and ads on free stuff.

—For other methods, get an up-to-date book on increasing traffic to your site.

Other uses for your site

Use your site to feed the media. Reporters want information fast. You can provide it fast by sending them to special web pages. E-mail newsworthy story ideas to specific reporters who have covered your issue in the past, and include a clickable web address that takes them to additional info on your website. Provide 72 dpi images that support your story, with links to 300 dpi high-quality jpegs for print publication.

You can also scan leaked documents and put them up as pdfs.

Combine e-mailed action alerts and web content. If you have a large list of supporters, consider using e-mailed action alerts that include a web address where people can go for more information. An action alert is a short clear statement of a problem that needs urgent attention. Be sure to include details of an action people can do immediately, such as sending a fax to a politician.

10.5   Direct Action

Direct action is good for small groups because it avoids the scourge of meeting-as-action. The benefit-to-cost ratio of direct action is high when it takes little time or resources and produces immediate concrete results.

Many practices attributed to good government started as direct actions by citizens unable to get any help from government. An example is traffic calming. It arose as a citizens' initiative in the Dutch town of Delft in the 1960s. Residents had appealed in vain to local government for measures that would stop cars from speeding through their neighborhood.

When a number of children were injured, locals took matters into their own hands by angle parking their cars on alternate sides of the street. Traffic had to slow down to weave around the parked cars. Local government tried to force residents to open up the street, but residents stood their ground and eventually placed heavy planters at the leading edge of each group of parked cars.

Boycotts

A boycott is one of the first ideas that comes up when groups are trying to put the screws on a corporation, but boycotts often don't work. Before launching a boycott campaign, carefully analyze the corporation, its marketing, profit margin, ownership, and customers.

A good target for a boycott is a well-known brand for which there is a ready alternative. For a small group, a good target is a local business engaged in some kind of unsavory practice. A poor target is one that can easily ignore any action you might dream up.

Shareholder activism

Recently activists have sought to change corporate practices from the inside by filing shareholder resolutions. In Canada, if you have held at least 2,000 shares of a public company for at least six months you have the right to file a resolution that will make it onto proxy ballots at the company's annual general meeting. If you do it right, you can get the company talking before the resolution hits the boardroom. Most high-level executives will try to frustrate you in hopes you will go away. If you don't go away, the company will often make concessions. This is especially true for initiatives that focus on sensitive and potentially embarrassing topics such as protecting the environment, eliminating child labor, and instituting legitimate accounting practices.

Most successful shareholder campaigns try to get the support of churches, social movement organizations, and other socially responsible investors, ethical investment funds, and large institutional investors. Successful campaigns also use media advocacy to try to create a climate that makes it difficult for the company to avoid making the "right" decision. In Canada the Social Investment Organization publishes an on-line handbook for shareholder activists at *www.socialinvestment.ca*. In the US, Friends of the Earth has a similar on-line handbook at *www.foe.org*. As well, the Interfaith Center on Corporate Responsibility offers many print publications on shareholder campaigns.

Personal funding

With personal funding, you decide what action would be effective; then fund it.

In North America, many people are shocked that anyone would spend their own money on a public interest project. "You shouldn't have to pay for that!" they say. "I hope you are going to be reimbursed!" But no one blinks an eye at self-indulgent purchases of luxury goods for private use.

The view that government or charities should pay for public goods ultimately means that many worthwhile things never get done. This is especially true of worthwhile projects deemed too "radical" for the usual sources of public interest funding. These don't stand a chance unless individuals contribute, because foundations are almost always too conservative, corporations are almost always too self-serving, and governments are almost always too worried about adverse public reaction.

Public demonstrations

In the June 2001 issue of *Social Forces,* Jackie Smith, John D. McCarthy, and others examine how public demonstrations in Washington DC attracted media coverage of social movement issues. They found that most media coverage focused on the protest *event,* rather than the issues that organizers wanted to highlight. Here is a summary of their findings:

—When demonstrations included violence, arrests, or counter-demonstrations, coverage was twice as likely to focus on the event rather than issues. The dilemma for protesters is how to attract media attention without the standby of visible conflict. Most protests in Washington, where protests are a daily occurrence, were not covered at all.

—Electronic sources were eight times more likely than print sources to report on issues behind demonstrations!

—When demonstrations focused on issues that were already part of media agendas, they received between two and five times more issue-oriented coverage.

—Stories relying on neutral sources or authorities were almost three times more likely to provide an extensive discussion of issues. Stories that relied on movement sources resisted presenting a movement perspective by devoting less space to issues.

—Stories about economic conflicts were half as likely to focus on issues and half as likely to receive a news spin favoring protesters as were stories on other topics.

The authors conclude that the factors that determine coverage of issue-oriented news were largely outside the control of social movement actors. They confirm that protests are still important for promoting internal solidarity and commitment among movement adherents.

But when it comes to making an issue part of the public agenda and a focus for media attention, the authors suggest that social movement groups communicate directly with other groups in society. They suggest that activists make their views available by talking to citizens groups, business organizations. schools, and church groups. As well, they suggest bypassing the mainstream media by focusing on grassroots media, books, newsletters, video documentaries, e-mail lists, listservs, websites, and internet-based news services such as Indy Media.

Mass actions

A mass action is any ordinary activity that becomes extraordinary when a lot of people do it at the same time in the same place. A mass action temporarily disrupts everyday routines in order to call attention to a problem. A familiar mass action involves a large group of people on bicycles filling the street at a specific time and place, then riding to a particular destination. It calls attention to a central problem for cities: The worst form of transportation has the most access to the street.

There are many other possibilities for mass actions: building occupations, land occupations, overloading of public facilities, picketing, various kinds of strikes, walkouts, deliberate inefficiency, mass shouts, marches and blockades, sit-downs, stand-ups, mock funerals, group silences, mass reporting sick, procotts (mass patronizing of an alternative), hartal (temporary cessation of economic activity), access blocking, and shareholder revolts for publicly traded companies.

Public Projections

Sometimes the best way to get your message out is to make it big and put it where everyone can see it. Unfortunately, most small non-profits can't afford billboards or huge signs. An alternative is text and image projected after dark on any large light-colored surface. An ordinary slide projector will do the job if you can get close enough to your projection surface. You can also use a carousel projector to rapidly project a series of slides. This adds movement that will draw people's attention. You might consider using a narrative text-image-text-image sequence.

The main problem with projections is that ambient light from street-lamps will often make a projected image weak. Test your site by projecting a slide at various distances from your screen. Keep in mind that the brightest view of the image will be from directly in front. The test will tell you if streetlights are a problem. If they are, you might be able to stick a piece of aluminum foil on the lamp housing to block spill in the direction of your image. You can use a long pole to hoist a piece of foil with double-sided tape attached. A more permanent alternative is to paint the light with a paint pad on a long pole.

Once you have a location, you need to decide what to project. A good choice is text that ridicules someone in power. Keep it short; four words is the max if you want to project a single line of large type and have one projector. Print the text out on a laser printer;

then photograph it with a high-contrast black-and-white copy film like Kodak Tech Pan.

Ask the photofinisher to develop the film only, then mount the negatives in slide mounts. The results projected will produce strong white type with no background.

You can project from a rooftop if you have a makeshift weather cover and a timer to turn the projector on and off. Or you can rearview project through a large window in a house or store. Make a roll-down screen for this purpose from a roll-down blind and use inexpensive, translucent, rearview projection film, available from suppliers that provide equipment for live theater. The advantage of a rearview setup is that the projector is inside, safe from tampering and the weather.

Billboard Improvement

Public space is a commons that should not be polluted with huge advertising messages. Many communities have sign control bylaws that prohibit billboards, but many do not, especially those that have succumbed to market forces or the lure of public-private partnerships. If your community is besmirched with billboards, you can treat their commercial culture as raw material for public entertainment. For instance, you can use a billboard detoucher to add acne to the faces of perfect fashion models – an action that reverses the photo retouching process common to fashion advertising. The detoucher is easily constructed by attaching a red oil stick to an L-bracket taped to the end of a ten-foot pole. Quickly banging the stick against the billboard produces waterproof zits.

Break minor laws

With so many laws in place, just about any activity out of the norm faces a law prohibiting it. In action planning sessions, some groups welcome minor lawbreaking ideas because it encourages creative thinking.

If your group actually decides to implement an action that goes beyond the letter of the law, you'll need to:

- get another opinion by running ideas past a direct action advocate outside your group,
- research actions and settings thoroughly,
- plan for every "what if" contingency,

- carry out activities quickly,
- make controversial alterations to public property small or temporary, and
- take appropriate security precautions.

For all actions you will want to check out sites beforehand so you know the amount of traffic at the site, escape routes, and what kind of lighting is present. For security at minor actions you should have two lookouts with portable CB or FM radios linked to the main perpetrator. Hide the lookouts or they will look suspicious. Limit radio use to emergencies and use coded language.

For more significant lawbreaking you will need to agree on measures to ensure the anonymity of participants, as well as measures to prevent bragging and storytelling after the action. You should also take steps to prevent infiltration and electronic surveillance by authorities. Find a guide to "security culture" and check out the detailed security measures in *EcoDefense: A Field Guide to Monkeywrenching*, edited by Dave Foreman and Bill Haywood.

In most cases, a little inventiveness will generate more effective alternatives to serious lawbreaking.

10.6   Extreme Versions of Direct Action

This book isn't the place to spell out the options for direct action that result in physical harm to people or severe damage to property. Because physical harm or threats of harm to people are counterproductive in democratic countries, most direct action advocates are careful to recommend *non-violent* direct action. When an event has the potential for violence, organizers have found it helps to have participants explicitly commit to non-violence beforehand

Under certain circumstances, damage to property can serve a purpose. The best-known advocate of direct action property damage is probably Paul Watson. He and the crew of the *Sea Shepherd* have rammed and sunk many ships involved in unlawful whaling. Even Watson's critics admit his actions have brought international and economic pressure to bear on illegal whalers and the countries that harbor them.

The best-known manual for property damage is *EcoDefense: A Field Guide to Monkeywrenching*. The book is full of instructions and diagrams on how to damage machinery used to harm the environment. The editors say that those involved in environmental destruction will only stop when it becomes too expensive to continue. Those objecting to extreme versions of direct action should read Dave Foreman's *Confessions of an Ecowarrior.*

Living it

Another form of extreme direct action is one that requires a full-time commitment from participants. A famous example is the Greenham Common Women's Peace Camp that carried out round-the-clock vigils for nineteen years at entrances to American airbases where planes carried nuclear-tipped cruise missiles. Their action was so compelling that by 1983 there were 24-hour peace camps set up outside *every* American airbase in Britain. The authority of the women of Greenham Common and others who "live it" comes from their commitment and authenticity, not from being experts on their subject.

Opportunities for direct action

Because direct action is viewed as radical, it has few advocates. But you can have a great deal of fun dreaming up and carrying out new and elegantly effective actions. To be effective they need to achieve an objective in themselves or connect to some larger strategy. Here are some examples of direct actions.

Guerrilla gardening. See 4.2 "Guerrilla gardening."

Stream clearing, stream minding. See also 5.1 "River guardians."

A safe injection site for drug users. A citizens' version can nudge government into setting up a "legitimate" safe injection site.

Tree spiking. Large nails driven into trees dull expensive saw blades. Only one person has ever been injured as a result of tree spiking, and that was because the spike was inserted parallel to the blade path, after the tree was cut down. Activists with a sense of theater don't do tree spiking. They prefer to perch in old-growth trees that are about to be cut.

Printing a newspaper parody. Usually both sides of a single sheet are printed. The front is a news parody that looks just like the local newspaper; the inside highlights the unreported facts about an issue. Activists hand them out at transit stations and wrap them around real newspapers in vending boxes.

Posting fake official notices. Government documents is easy to find. With a little care it is easy to use them to create fake official notices, fake polls, fake studies, fake bills and tickets.

Bumper stickers. Owner-applied stickers have disappeared as bumpers are now painted. But fly posters are still an option, like the one intended for SUVs: "I'm changing the climate"; or the one intended for sports cars: "I'd rather have a bigger dick." A fly poster is a sign applied to a site without the owner's permission.

T-shirts. A T-shirt with a good headline can become an effective public interest ad. Your group can create its own shirts now that many inexpensive color printers will produce iron-on transfers. This is a good alternative to the T-shirt with a corporate logo. You advertise your ideas instead of their products.

Badges. Make your own with a color printer, card paper or photographic paper, a safety pin, and tape. Can't get it just right? Nab a catchy headline, graph, graphic, or photo from a newspaper or public interest publication.

Printing money. Designing and printing money can be part of a declaration of local independence, or the formation of a new city state such as the Peoples Republic of East Vancouver. It can also be part of a genuine local currency system, a LETSystem (Local Exchange Trading System), or a local money system like Ithaca Hours. The web has plenty of information on LETSystems. A good book on all systems is *Money: Understanding and Creating Alternatives to Legal Tender* by Thomas Greco.

Posting tiny fly posters in public places. Place stickers with unsettling facts at eye level where people come up close, such as office building doors, mall doors, bank machines, backs of bus seats, public telephones, washroom dividers, or street poles with a crosswalk button.

Renaming streets, renaming institutions. Residents in a neighborhood may choose a more appropriate name or reactivate a historic name for a street or institution. For instance, Brewery Creek ran through a neighborhood in early Vancouver. The creek provided water for three breweries and a soft drink plant. Years later, it was later filled in and replaced by a street called Scotia. Residents might decide a better name for the street would be Brewery. They could erect their own signs and use the name in information about the neighborhood.

Guerrilla theatre. Small groups can stage guerrilla theatre events to draw attention to their point of view. When Barclay's Bank in England invested over £6 million in South African Defense Bonds in the 1970s, an anti-apartheid group arranged for two people to dress up in South African military uniforms and parade in front of Barclay's headquarters. Students at Tulane University used guerrilla theatre in 1972 to protest Richard Nixon's support of the Vietnam war at a speech the president made at the university. They dressed up as members of the Ku Klux Klan, applauded loudly whenever Nixon said anything in support of the war, and waved placards saying "The KKK supports Nixon."

Mass loudspeaking. Some groups equip protesters with a small, inexpensive, portable amps and speakers to make one very large sound system. Each has a tiny FM receiver so the unit will pick up broadcasts from a simple FM transmitter located nearby. See "Radio Broadcasting" below. Another way to amplify sound is with a 12-volt amp that plugs into a car cigarette lighter. A sound truck is even better.

Banner hanging. Ruckus and Greenpeace run training camps that show activists how to climb bridges and buildings in order to hang huge banners. For more info see *ruckus.org*.

Continuous crosswalking. Residents fed up with commuter traffic roaring through their neighborhood can block a major arterial during rush hour by arranging for a steady stream of people to use a pedestrian crosswalk. This technique is an example of dislocation: the creative deployment of human bodies.

Homemade speed bumps. Nail a 2 x 6 to the road with concrete nails, then watch the cars slow down.

Creative potholing. Dig holes in the streets to slow traffic. Renting a jackhammer helps.

Moving furniture onto residential streets. This slows down traffic and is a good way to meet your neighbors. See 4.4 "Street Reclaiming."

Tunneling under development sites. Activists create shallow tunnels under land they are trying to protect. They move in and inform the authorities, who then have to dig them out before machinery can enter the site. A safer version of this British technique is to replace people with people-sized sacks of silage, which fool detectors because they give off heat.

Creating and airing a newspaper or TV ad. For an ad to be effective, your target audience needs to see it more than once. This can be expensive. To keep the cost down, create a "micro-ad" for newspapers or produce a 30-second TV ad for airing late at night. Another angle is to air your ad during unpopular (less expensive) shows watched by your target audience. You can also create an ad and then pitch it to a group of wealthy progressives in hopes they will contribute enough cash to place the ad.

Subvertising on cars. Get your message out with a hinged sandwich board mounted on your roof rack or a large vinyl magnet sign attached to the side of your vehicle.

Painting images or messages on sidewalks. Use a stencil and clear exterior polyurethane. It makes a mark that disappears in the rain.

Pie throwing. The recipe for successful pie throwing involves several key ingredients: the target's itinerary, careful planning, proximity, the element of surprise, and an abundance of pies and throwers. Many people feel that pie throwing is too abusive, even for people who abuse the public trust.

Effigy burning. There are variations; you can burn other things. You can also crush, stuff, hurl, dissolve, vaporize, remodel, dismantle, sink, and so forth.

Protecting heritage buildings. See 4.1 "Heritage home guard."

Radio broadcasting. Low-power transmitters are simple and inexpensive, and there are many ways radio transmitters can be used. For instance, if you set them up at demonstrations and rallies, motorists can tune their radios to a frequency displayed on large banners and listen in on what is happening. For how-to information go to *www.radio4all.org*.

Modifying rented videotapes. Subvertisers can replace the ads at the beginning of rented videotapes with their own video, or stills from a digital camera. To record, simply place a piece of tape over the hole that is covered by a plastic tab on blank videotapes.

Staging impromptu street parties. In the 1990s the English group Reclaim the Streets staged happenings that took over public space. John Jordan describes one of these in *DiY Culture:*

> *Imagine a busy high street, Saturday afternoon. Shoppers mingle on the thin strip of pavement that separates shops from the busy road. Suddenly two cars careen into each other and block the road: the drivers get out and begin to argue. One of the drivers brandishes a hammer and starts to smash up the other driver's car. The other driver retaliates with a hammer attack of his own. Passersby are astonished; time stands still. Then people surge out of the anonymous shopping crowd and start to jump on top of the cars. Multicolored*

paint is thrown everywhere. An enormous banner is unfurled from the roofs of the two destroyed vehicles. RECLAIM THE STREETS – FREE THE CITY / KILL THE CAR, it proclaims. Five hundred people are now surging out of the tube station and take over the street. As the Surrealists might have said, everyday life has been penetrated by the marvelous.

No one can say what the prospects are for growing the grassroots and improving citizen action. But one thing is certain: the future looks bright. Translating *The Troublemaker's Teaparty* into action will help. No revolution is needed, just a small increase in the number of involved citizens and a little improvement in their ability to get things done. The result will be everyday life "penetrated by the marvelous."

NICK COBBING

Los Angeles Bus Riders Union

Appendix 1

How the IAF Organizes

THE INDUSTRIAL AREAS FOUNDATION (IAF) probably does the best grass-roots organizing in the US. Legendary organizer Saul Alinsky set up the IAF in the 1970s to train organizers, see 10.2 "Rules for Radicals". It still emphasizes the training of organizers, but it has shed some of its confrontational approach and adopted one more focused on negotiation and compromise as a better way to meet the needs of low-income people. The IAF has been instrumental in increasing wages, providing housing, and improving schools in poor neighborhoods. This is not the place to spell out the IAF's accomplishments. But it is worthwhile summarizing a number of highly successful IAF methods that differ from those usually found in community organizing. Anyone interested in a more complete rendering of IAF practices should read Mark Warren's excellent book *Dry Bones Rattling: Community Building to Revitalize American Democracy*.

Because the IAF organizes on a large scale, some of what it does will not make sense for small unfunded groups. But the IAF's approach to organizing and many of its tactics will help small groups become more effective.

The IAF organizes through church networks.
Much IAF organizing occurs through Christian churches, particularly the Catholic church. Because of this, it is often called faith-based organizing. The IAF taps existing parish networks to find the people it needs to achieve its goals. (This approach resembles the way successful social movements co-opt existing communications networks; see Appendix 2). In Texas, the IAF obtained the support of the bishop, who then encouraged parishes to join the foundation. The congregations of these parishes contribute dues to the IAF and volunteer for IAF campaigns.

If community organizing through churches seems unusual, remember that not so long ago church and community were intimately intertwined. Every community of place was also a community of faith.

Despite the strong focus on church networks, the IAF is working to broaden its organizing. It has begun developing relationships with secular institutions such as schools, health care providers, and unions.

The IAF tries to bond self-interest with core values.
It appeals to self-interest to bring in participants, but it recognizes that participation will rise and fall with issues if only based on self-interest. Thus the IAF tries to engage people by linking self-interest with core values. It does this by framing campaign actions in terms of important stories and cultural symbols. For Christian groups the IAF links campaign actions to stories from the Old and New Testament. For Jewish groups it chooses important Jewish stories; for labor groups, stories of important labor struggles.

Tapping church networks solves the mobilization problem
For many community organizations a recurring problem is getting people out for an action. An intimate link to a network of people who attend church every week makes this much easier. A common IAF action is an accountability night when IAF leaders extract commitments from politicians standing at the front of the room. Churches can deliver thousands of people for accountability nights because parish priests explain the reason for the action and encourage members of their congregations to attend.

The IAF tries to identify and train as many natural leaders as possible.
In modern egalitarian society the recent trend has been to downplay leaders and create flat organizations with no clear lines of authority. This works for small groups, but larger organizations often wind up being run by small cliques. Then anything can happen. Because cliques have no formal authority there is nothing to hold them accountable.

In IAF terms, a leader is anyone who has, and can consistently deliver, a following. Leaders have to commit in advance to bring a certain number of people to public actions and accountability nights for elected officials. Organizers count heads and actually hold leaders responsible for meeting their quotas.

The IAF has three tiers of leaders. Tertiary leaders are usually parish members who bring friends, family, neighbors, and work associates to IAF actions. With this approach the IAF formalizes the usual way most people get involved: a friend or family member asks them to take part.

Secondary leaders are the leaders of member institutions, often pastors or influential parishioners. They are more involved in particular action campaigns and in meeting the needs of their own organizations. They also meet in an assembly every few months to ratify the decisions of an executive committee made up of the most experienced "primary" leaders. Secondary leaders are expected to deliver a following from their institution. As well, they must commit to the IAF training process.

Organizers identify potential leaders by holding 30-minute one-on-one meetings with candidates referred by the lead organizer or a top leader. According to Ernesto Cortes, director of IAF's southwest region, organizers look for a clear sense of self-interest in getting involved, a willingness to act, and the presence of controlled or "cold" anger. They also look for a sense of humor, imagination, maturity, risk-taking, responsibility, aggressiveness, integrity, and a healthy ego. Because the IAF always needs more leaders, every effort is made to draw identified leaders into the organization.

Paid professional organizers train leaders; leaders conduct campaigns

The IAF is famous for its "iron rule": Never do for people what they can do for themselves. Applied to organizing it means that staff organizers should train leaders how to run an action campaign, not do it themselves. In practice, organizers often assist leaders. This way they help the leaders to grow and avoid the risk of costly mistakes.

The staff of most other community groups conduct campaigns themselves and give little time to developing new leaders. As a result, their member base shrinks. By making the focus of staff the recruitment and training of leaders, the IAF continually expands its member base.

The IAF appeals to the self-interest of its leaders

In Texas, a third of primary leaders are clergy; the remaining two-thirds are middle-aged women from poor and working-class congregations in communities of color. Lay leaders are inspired to volunteer their time, first to make tangible improvements to their lives; second to act on a deep religious caring for community; and third to take advantage of opportunities for personal growth and the potential to become a "mover and shaker." By emphasizing training, and by using campaigns as real-life workshops, the IAF places far more emphasis on personal growth than most community groups. Personal growth and the ability to wield power is particularly exciting for low-income women, for whom this is a new experience.

Over the long term, those who remain involved with the IAF are motivated by a belief they are doing "God's work," as well as by concern for their community and "cold anger" at the injustice it has had to suffer.

The IAF emphasizes praxis over action

Praxis is practice grounded in knowledge combined with reflection and evaluation. According to Ernesto Cortes, the most important part is the reflection and evaluation that follows an action. This takes place in group meetings with other leaders. It also takes place in more candid one-on-one meetings with organizers. Here organizers will often agitate and challenge leaders to learn and develop. The objective is to overcome obstacles that block a leader's growth. This kind of strong personal tutoring is unheard of in other kinds of citizen's groups.

The IAF uses campaign evaluations for personal development

Most community organizations do project evaluations, but they are quick, cursory, and impersonal. The IAF version is more formal, but it's also deeper and more personal. At 10-day national training sessions, the IAF devotes a full day to the analysis of each person's self-interest. Trainers steer participants toward a relational rather than personal view of self-interest, since a person's interests form in a context of relationships with others.

So many community-based efforts run into trouble because they allow campaign objectives to sideline the self-interest of participants. It's worth taking time to align public interest objectives with participants' self-interest. The exercise deepens the commitment to pubic action and avoids competition between public and private life.

The IAF uses personal stories to forge alliances

The IAF's approach is often called "relational organizing" because organizers spend a lot of time teaching leaders how to build relationships within and between organizations. To build relationships between organizations the IAF tries to develop strong personal ties between people from different organizations, as well as from different races and different income levels. To do this it brings leaders from different organizations together in small groups where they share personal stories and engage in "deep listening." People are encouraged to speak about important experiences that have shaped their lives. The process is not a quick preamble that precedes "getting down to business"; it *is* the business and often takes place over many days. Sharing life experiences creates an intimate bond between different people and develops the trust that is necessary for intergroup cooperation.

The IAF's use of personal stories and deep listening is not unique. It is practiced in traditional cultures; it also resembles M. Scott Peck's approach to building deep community described in *Different Drum*, See 2.2 "Deep Community".

Sharing personal stories does more than create bridges between different groups of people. When leaders understand and share their own stories, it clears the way for candid reflection following an action that will contribute to a leader's growth. Sharing personal stories also helps to bond personal and public interest.

For many reasons, most citizens groups don't engage in this kind of work. Most focus on devising actions, not on building relationships. Most spend no time at all building relationships with people outside their own · circle. Many feel that telling personal stories is too personal, too much like group therapy. But pragmatic groups should consider the practice because it works. Developing deep relationships between the leaders of different parts of civil society breeds a willingness to cooperate that makes it much easier to get things done. Relational organizing appears to be one of the best ways to bridge the many disconnected parts of civil society. It also seems to be a way of facilitating the partnership arrangements advocated by John McKnight and John Kretzmann in *Building Communities from the Inside Out.*

The IAF mixes consensus with decision making by leaders
The IAF believes people operate and should operate through leadership. The most experienced leaders make most of the decisions at the IAF, leaving less experienced leaders and the rank and file to ratify these decisions at regular assemblies. The process usually goes smoothly because agreements on contentious issues are worked out by informal consensus before formal ratification meetings. In fact, IAF leaders spend a lot of informal time reasoning with one another to reach a consensus that will be supported.

IAF leaders are chosen through a similar process. They are recommended rather than elected, and then are chosen through informal discussion and consensus amongst top leaders before being ratified at an assembly or larger convention.

The IAF tries to prevent cliques.
The IAF warns leaders about limiting friendships that seem to be coalescing around a clique. Cliques get in the way of broad-based relationships that cut across diverse communities.

No permanent political ties.
The IAF maintains a strictly non-partisan position so that it can work with people on the right or the left or anywhere in between.

House meetings link to the grassroots.
The IAF will often ask its network of leaders to invite friends and neighbors to their houses to discuss a particular issue, such as how to provide job training for low-income wage earners. These conversations, which include people directly affected by the issue, are intended to find a basis for action on a problem. The conversations also provide personal stories that are collected for later use in motivating others.

Research meetings create allies.
The IAF combines the bottom-up approach of house meetings with the top-down approach of research meetings with experts and business and public officials. Research meetings create allies, add credibility, and help to define the details of public policy initiatives. It's worth noting that research meetings are face-to-face meetings. The IAF rightly believes that the art of politics is best conducted in person, not by telephone, letter, or e-mail.

When the foundation wanted to create a job-training program for low-income residents in San Antonio, IAF leaders met with local business and found there were not enough workers to fill certain well-paid jobs.

They met with community college representatives to identify program possibilities. They met with city politicians. They met with other IAF groups in the state to identify opportunities for cross-network collaboration. They met with state and local experts on labor force development. In addition, they met with a number of national labor force economists who could make suggestions and would endorse the training initiative that followed.

The IAF recognizes the importance of resources.
Most IAF affiliates have an annual budget of around $150,000, enough to pay at least one organizer, cover office staff and organizational overhead, and pay the cost of extensive leader training. About 20 percent comes from dues, 20 percent from the Catholic Campaign for Human Development, 30 percent from private foundations and corporations, and the rest from local fundraising and other faith-based funders. Like most progressive organizations, the IAF's activities are limited by the resources it can mobilize. For more on the impact of resources see Appendix 2.

Many IAF practices could help grow the grassroots by improving the health and competence of groups both large and small. Particularly important is the way the IAF focuses on how much participants learn as opposed to how much the group accomplishes.

Appendix 2

Social Movements:
A Summary of What Works

WHAT AFFECTS THE SUCCESS of social movements? What do the civil liberties, feminist, environmental, gay rights, anti-nuke, gun control, don't drink and drive, and living wage movements have in common? Since the 1960s a small number of sociologists have been conducting research, trying to answer this question. Research on social movements complements the limited, often personal, perspective of activists and organizers because it looks at larger numbers of people, longer periods of time, and major shifts in popular attitudes.

Little of this work, known as the resource mobilization perspective of social movements, has made its way out of universities. What follows is an attempt to make this work available to a larger audience by presenting it in simple language. Appendix 2 summarizes and updates a detailed review article "Social Movements," by Doug McAdam, John D. McCarthy, and Mayer Zald, originally published in the *Handbook of Sociology*, edited by Neil Smelser. The empirical approach of McAdam, McCarthy and Zald is distinct from the more theoretical approach to social movements preferred by European intellectuals like Jurgen Habermas, which focuses on symbolic production and cultural conflict.

McAdam, McCarthy, and Zald identify three factors critical to social movements: political opportunity, organizational capacity, and framing ability. They look at social movements as politics by other means, often the only means open to relatively powerless challenging groups. They argue for the constancy of discontent and claim that higher levels of resources rather than higher levels of discontent best account for the emergence and development of insurgency.

Here is a summary of what contributes to the birth, maintenance, and success of social movements.

Favorable Pre-conditions

Elements and conditions that contribute to the rise of a social movement.

Individual psychology is not so important. Early work on social movements assumed that activism could be explained by examining the psychological motivations of individuals. A popular theory was that activism came from a perceived gap between what a person felt he or she was entitled to and what he or she actually received. Research shows that individual predispositions are insufficient to account for participation in collective action.

Prosperity. Prosperity affords the resources necessary for social movements. Other things being equal, the most deprived seem unable to sustain more than momentary insurgency. Money also makes a difference to local, short-term initiatives; wealthy neighborhoods are much better than poor neighborhoods at getting concessions from local government.

Physical concentration. Bringing people into close proximity in cities, factories, and university campuses increases the potential for social movement activity. The civil rights movement followed the mass migration of blacks from dispersed rural settlements to concentrated urban centers in the US South. Short-lived instances of physical concentration also foment social change. Conferences, for instance, often energize participants to pursue progressive change. Sports events, carnivals, and concerts have less predictable outcomes.

Level of prior grassroots organization. Already existing church groups, clubs, special interest organizations, teams and recreational groups, community groups, PTAs, veterans, and educational organizations support the development of social movements. The early stages of mobilization can be difficult if most people lead purely private lives, and if grassroots groups have few members.

The absence of cross-cutting solidarities. It is easier for a movement to grow in a population that is isolated or has weak ties to other groups in society. The feminist movement initially encountered a good deal of resistance from married women in the US because these women had a wide variety of social and economic ties to men.

Suddenly imposed grievances, dramatic spotlighting. Dramatic, highly publicized, unexpected events can lead to public outrage and major shifts in public attitudes. Huge oil spills, nuclear accidents, revelations of serious government misconduct, official violence against dissenters, or the sudden loss of employment serve to foment social movement.

Solidarity instead of free riding. Many sociologists have argued that social movements are hampered by the tendency for people to do a quick cost-benefit analysis of their participation. Rational people will conclude the easiest course is to become a free rider, since they will obtain the benefits of social action whether they participate or not.

To address free-rider absenteeism, smart activists emphasize solidarity, personal relationships, and the importance of individual commitment for success. Established organizations with paid organizers are much better equipped to address the free-rider issue. See also "Grassroots Wilt 10: The catch-22 of collective action."

Individual Inducements

Factors that motivate people to join a social movement.

Prior contact with a movement member. Research shows the strongest inducement to activism is prior contact with a movement member. For instance, new recruits to peace movements are typically people already associated with members of peace groups.

Membership in many organizations. Another indicator of individual activism is the number of organizations a person belongs to. Because of the difficulty of recruiting isolated individuals, most organizers target members of organizations that might be sympathetic to their cause.

Prior activism. People who have previously been involved in some form of collective action in their past are more likely to be involved in collective action in the future. Having learned the role of activist, it is easier to adopt the role again. The longer one spends in the role of activist, the more integral it becomes to one's identity.

Availability. Life circumstances affect participation by affecting availability. People with full-time jobs, marriages, and family responsibilities are less likely to participate in social movement activity. Autonomous individuals with few personal responsibilities, such as college students and single professionals, are more likely participants.

Emotional tension. People are more likely to act collectively when responding to strong emotions. Community organizers typically try to identify an emotional issue that will motivate people to participate. The Chinese students who drove the 1989 democracy movement in China were spurred by a roller coaster of strong emotions. It started with grief and anger over the murder of Hu Yaobang, the sympathetic general secretary of the Communist Party; continued with a heroic hunger strike accompanied by vows of self-sacrifice; and ended with fear and hopeful exhilaration brought on by the risky defiance of martial law, and the blockading of entrances to the city.

Moving music. Music is often central to the rise of a social movement. Music can stir people up because it speaks to the emotions better than pictures or words. Tom Paine, a hero of the American Revolution, wrote new lyrics for popular folk tunes as a way of attacking the British. Historians frequently mention the importance of Tom Paine's pamphlets, but overlook his music. In the last century, music has been central to the labor movement, the civil rights movement, and the movement to end the war in Vietnam. For more on the influence of music see *Rockin' the Boat* by Reebee Garofalo.

The Ingredients of Micro-mobilization
The links between social movements and small groups.

Kindling in small groups. The basic building block of social movements is the small informal group connected to a loose network. Sometimes this "micro-mobilization context" is a small group of friends, sometimes a group of co-workers, sometimes a subgroup within a larger group like a church or a union. A well-known example of a small group is the four Greensboro A&T students who precipitated the 1960s black sit-in movement after "bull sessions" in one another's dorm rooms.

Familiar members. Small groups act as the staging ground for movements. Three resources affect the emergence of a movement: members, leaders, and an existing communications network. Research shows that new members tend to know people who are already members. The more a person is integrated into an activist community, the more readily he or she will be willing to take part in protest activities.

Capable leaders. Smart, honest, committed leaders are invaluable to a social movement. The literature on activism emphasizes the importance of leaders in generating a movement, and the importance of creating new leaders to keep it rolling. Particularly important is the articulate and charismatic leader who can elegantly articulate everyone's concerns and inspire an emotional response.

Supportive celebrities – rock stars, famous actors, big-name athletes, well-known authors – while not true leaders, can give a movement currency and profile amongst audiences of normally uninvolved "bystanders."

A co-optable communications network. The pattern, speed, and spread of a movement depends on the existence of a co-optable communications network that links people through a combination of regular conferences and workshops; dedicated magazines, newspapers or newsletters; and e-mail bulletins. The greater the number and diversity of people actively participating in a network, the more likely it will support a mobilization effort. The women's liberation movement was able to make rapid progress in the 1960s (when it had previously failed to do so) because of the prior arrival of such a network. After 1967, the news that women were organizing spread like a chain reaction through numerous underground newspapers and New Left conferences.

Networks can also be informal and invisible, like those described in detail in Emanuel Rosen's book, *The Anatomy of Buzz*. Rosen sees networks as useful for flogging products; activists see them as useful for spreading ideas. Activists could learn something from books on social networks, viral marketing, and the spread of epidemics. Because social movements seem to spread like other innovations, activists might also learn something from the literature on technical and cultural diffusion, and the role of early adopters.

A mobilizing frame. Erving Goffman came up with the term "frame" to refer to an interpretive scheme that people use to simplify and make sense of some aspect of the world. When a mobilizing frame becomes widely shared, the chances of collective action increase markedly.

Corporations and the corporate media try to preserve the status quo by promoting demobilizing frames. These frames blame the victim by linking unfortunate events to individual shortcomings (see Appendix 3). They promote the view that lung cancer results from consumer choice, unemployment from laziness, and family breakup from selfishness. A movement can build quickly inside a homogenous, highly interactive group when people question the blame-the-victim frame and begin to see that a problem arises not from flawed individuals, but from flawed public policy.

Frame alignment. Frame alignment describes what happens in small informal groups that promote social change. Movement supporters attempt to recruit bystanders by providing examples and rationales that support a mobilizing frame and legitimize the movement. If the examples and rationale are convincing, bystanders will adjust their view of issues and events to fit the new mobilizing frame.

Most frame alignment comes from social movement organizations as they try to bring in new people and fend off countermovement attacks. Frame alignment comes in many varieties. One example is frame extension. According to David Snow and others, frame extension occurs when a social movement organization extends "the boundaries of its primary framework so as to encompass interests or points of view that are incidental to its primary objectives but of considerable salience to potential adherents." In other words, it's about expanding objectives and activities in order to bring more people on board.

Optimistic expectations. Any given individual is more likely to participate in a project if he or she:
• expects a large number of people to participate,
• expects his/her participation will contribute to success, and
• expects success if many people participate.

The relentless enthusiasm of a good organizer will inspire enthusiasm and optimism in others, even in the worst circumstances.

Movement Maintenance
How larger, funded organizations contribute to a social movement.

The need for social movement organizations. Micro-mobilization spurs collective action, but informal groups of friends, ad hoc committees, or loose associations of activists are not sufficient to develop or maintain a movement. This requires social movement organizations or SMOs. Typically these "command posts of the movement" have an office, staff, volunteers, and a board of directors

Role of the SMO. A social movement organization needs to carve out a niche for itself in the larger environment of other organizations pursuing similar objectives. As well, it must develop productive relationships with media, funders, and government. Most importantly, each SMO must figure out a way to establish a regular flow of people and money to support the "cause." SMOs that demand the least from members will be the most successful in obtaining members and money. One common variation – the professional SMO – purports to speak for a large constituency, but consists of a small paid staff connected through direct mail to "members" who are little more than donors.

Radical flank effects. Research on SMOs pursuing relatively similar goals shows the presence of extremist groups leads to greater support for moderate groups. Funders increase their support to moderate groups as a way of undercutting radical groups. Moreover, the presence of more extreme groups alters the definition of the middle, making former radicals seem merely progressive. To secure their place, the new moderates have to denounce the actions of their extremist counterparts as irresponsible, immoral, and counterproductive. The most astute will quietly encourage "responsible extremism" at the same time.

Government control through regulation, intimidation, and co-optation. The modern state usually defends elite interests and resists social movements. It does so though tax policies; laws affecting boycotts, strikes, and blockades; strategic withholding of funds; denial of non-profit charity status; police intimidation; and various forms of co-optation.

The use of force is a dicey issue for government. In the short run, systematic, sustained, moderate force works. But if it goes on too long or becomes extreme, the use of force can generate a backlash against government and a boost for the movement. Because a violent response to a peaceful protest generates great sympathy from the media and the general public, peaceful provocation has become a standard tactic of activists. But protest organizers always face the problem of trying to control a small number of violent participants. If they fail, the media will portray this minority as representative of all protesters, making a violent response from government authorities seem justified.

In modern democracies, government control often amounts to co-optation or absorption. This can take the form of providing funds to potentially problematic groups, hiring activist leaders to positions in government, or appointing activists to boards. It can also take the form of what is called "symbolic reassurance," with governments setting up special hearings, commissions, or agencies to address a particular concern or grievance.

Government facilitation. Governments are not always on the other side. They will assist SMOs pursuing objectives in sync with their own, sometimes creating programs, conferences, and special funding to bolster the membership and credibility of their favorite SMO. When fears of public or corporate backlash stall progressive policy changes, they will support advocacy groups as a means of building public support. In Canada, the Non-Smokers Rights Coalition received millions of dollars from the federal government to publicly lobby for laws requiring cigarette packages to carry large text warnings and gruesome photos showing the damage caused by smoking. In effect, the feds paid to be openly lobbied in the media, then responded when the public began to see the need for government action.

SMOs often try to exploit circumstances where different levels of government (federal, provincial / state, municipal), or different departments within the same government, wind up on different sides of the same issue. In the American civil rights movement, federal laws and lawsuits clamped down on southern sheriffs and voting registrars. In one important move, US president Eisenhower called out the National Guard to constrain Arkansas governor Faubus during the Little Rock school desegregation crisis.

Occasionally groups can use the courts to advance a social movement. Juries can impede authority by nullifying formal law. Juries in Canada nullified the laws prohibiting abortion by repeatedly delivering not-guilty verdicts for doctors who performed abortions.

Court proceedings or semi-judicial hearings may also be able to capture media attention that will develop public support for movement goals. Still, a judicial route can cost a lot of time and money, even if a public interest advocate is willing to take the case pro bono. As a rule, the courts are good at preventing injustice but poor at furthering progress.

Consciousness maintaining. The widespread adoption of a mobilizing frame and recognition of the value of individual contributions to collective action may be sufficient to generate collective action but not enough to maintain it. The demise of radical feminism in the US, first after the Civil War and then after passage of the suffrage amendment, shows how tenuous political consciousness can be. To succeed, a movement must generate support from authorities and sympathy from bystanders and, most important, must continue to be seen as legitimate and effective by movement members. This inevitably means an ongoing struggle with movement opponents to frame events and issues in a way that supports the movement.

Most SMOs use media advocacy (Chapter 9) to maintain movement momentum. Ideally an SMO will be able to create an ongoing theatrical performance, with the public as a mass audience. This is much easier to achieve if the drama focuses on changes to the way people lead their lives rather than changes to institutions.

In their struggle for favorable public opinion, SMOs use various communications technologies to get their messages out. They use the telephone to recruit potential members, reconnect to lapsed members, and generate action alerts though established telephone trees. They use direct mail to reinforce movement frames, acquire resources, and foment direct action. Many SMOs also try to earn TV coverage because the effectiveness of direct mail fundraising improves dramatically with television exposure. Maintaining consciousness on a limited budget requires inventive communications. The most effective SMOs have top-notch communications professionals on staff.

Ongoing frame alignment. Sociologists take pains to point out that frame alignment only works as an ongoing process. When confronted with a challenge, an SMO must diagnose the problem in a way that resonates with members and potential members, propose a plausible solution that could be accomplished by movement participation, and issue a call to arms that motivates action. A successful SMO must also work hard to maintain the relevance of supportive frames while attacking, debunking, and ridiculing counterframes. Defensive measures usually include polarized us-versus-them framing and may go further to frame opponents' actions as self-serving or dishonest. Loss of alignment is a constant threat when members are subjected to the counterframes of opponents.

Frames from the news. Most people acquire their information and orientation to the world from the impersonal mass media. With it they acquire stock frames and frame-making ideologies. What they come to see as their own opinions for or against a social movement are actually constructed by the news. Right-wing ideology, for instance, is both news constructed and heavily promoted by the corporate owners of the mass media. It assumes that we suffer from too much government, too many taxes, and too many controls on corporate enterprise. Any ideology, once adopted by the mass media, will almost certainly infect the public that relies on the media for information. Only the most vigilant can resist this kind of consistent framing, story after story, day after day.

Oppositional frames from intellectual workers. Those who teach at universities and colleges generate frames and frame-making ideologies that counter established frames, including those of the mass media. Thus universities and colleges often serve as incubators for progressive movements. Many movements, however, never make it beyond the university gates. They are frequently abandoned by students who, on graduation, depart for a variety of milieus where countermovement frames prevail. Progressive social movements would certainly benefit from academics spending more time outside academe, talking to lay audiences in everyday language on radio, on TV, in op-eds, in workshops.

Resource maintenance. SMOs often face a dilemma when it comes to raising funds. If their members are impoverished and they depend on their members for funds, they will wind up spending an inordinate amount of time and energy on fundraising for very little return. If, on the other hand, they look to external elites, they will face funding uncertainties or strings attached. External support usually tames movements, steering them toward the more conservative goals of elite funders. Nevertheless, most social movements eventually turn to elites – foundations, corporations, and rich philanthropists – for assistance in order to sustain themselves long enough to obtain substantial victories. A few funders have tried to avoid taming the movements they support. The British Crossroads Fund has tried to do this with a board made up of both donors and activists who make decisions about grants.

Membership maintenance. Besides attracting resources and new recruits, a movement must strive to maintain the energies and loyalties of existing members. Like any effective small group, an effective SMO will focus on frame alignment, trying its best to ensure a fit between members' values and movement goals. It will also work for concrete action and visible victories, since people are drawn to a movement when they see it as a forum for action, and soon drop out if nothing happens.

SMOs goals and tactics. SMOs face an uphill battle simply surviving, let alone achieving substantive political, social, or economic change. They have in their arsenal two potentially powerful weapons: engaging goals and effective tactics. Unfortunately, many organizations are weak on strategic thinking and unfamiliar with social movement research. As a result, some engage in violent or abusive action, which attracts media attention but alienates supporters. This is what happened to Black Power groups in the 1960s. Other organizations, like the Sea Shepherd Society, succeed because they have found ways to legitimize violence in pursuit of their goals. On the question of goals, research shows the wisdom of maintaining a narrow focus and a single goal. SMOs pursuing a single goal are far more successful than those pursuing many goals.

Further Social Movement Research

This brief overview should not be seen as a recipe for creating a successful social movement, but as a basis for intelligent action in the ever-changing landscape of movement politics. Despite the importance of social movements, many questions remain unanswered:

- Can the ignition of a movement be carried out in organized fashion, or is it dependent on the arrival of the right conditions?
- What are the best practices for small groups that have no resources?
- Under what conditions can successful framing overcome a lack of structural capacity?
- How much time should activists spend developing frames that fuse personal and collective identities?
- What are the shortcomings of the resource mobilization view of social movements?

Appendix 3

Framing the News

Adapted from *Prime Time Activism: Media Strategies for Grassroots Organizing* by Charlotte Ryan, published by South End Press.

W E LIKE TO THINK of reality as fixed, as something we can all agree on. We realize the news media may make mistakes, but trust that they largely present reality "the way it is." The news media make every effort to promote this view by trying to appear neutral and objective. But the writers and editors who report the news are anything but objective. They construct a subjective picture of reality, selecting and organizing a confusing flood of information in a way that makes sense to themselves and their audiences. This process is called framing.

Struggles over framing decide which of the day's many happenings will be awarded significance. The media have become critical arenas for this struggle. Social movements have increasingly focused on the media since they play such an influential role in assigning importance to public issues. But gaining attention alone is not what a social movement wants. The real battle is over whose interpretation, whose framing of reality, gets the floor.

Most information we receive is already framed: friends offer opposing accounts of a feud; TV, radio, and newspapers interpret events that we do not experience directly. Even when we are actual witnesses, we are not privileged with the truth. Who we are – our class, gender, race, past experience, values, and interests – all come into play when we try to make sense of what's happening.

Yet it is common to downplay framing as a value-laden ordering process. Those of us who question the naturalness of the packaged world are ignored or attacked, rarely believed. This is because frames are not consciously or deliberately constructed, but operate as underlying mind-sets that prompt people to notice elements that are familiar and ignore those that are different. News frames are almost entirely implicit and taken for granted. They do not appear to either journalists or audience as social constructions but as primary attributes of events that reporters are merely reflecting. News frames make the world look natural. They determine what is selected, what is excluded, what is emphasized. In short, news presents a packaged world.

Far from being an objective list of facts, a news story results from multiple subjective decisions about whether and how to present happenings to media audiences. The editors' and reporters' own perspectives, including their notions of audience interests, guide this process. As a result, stories covering the same happening may vary dramatically. Consider the following hypothetical alternative versions of the same incident:

Version 1
Rats Bite Infant

An infant left sleeping in his crib was bitten repeatedly by rats while his 16-year-old mother went to cash her welfare check. A neighbor responded to the cries of the infant and brought the child to Central Hospital, where he was treated and released in his mother's custody. The mother, Angie Burns of the South End, explained softly, "I was only gone five minutes. I left the door open so my neighbor would hear him if he woke up. I never thought this would happen in the daylight."

Version 2
Rats Bite Infant – Landlord, Tenants Dispute Blame

An eight-month-old South End boy was treated and released from Central Hospital yesterday after being bitten by rats while he was sleeping in his crib. Tenants said that repeated requests for extermination had been ignored by the landlord, Henry Brown. Brown claimed that the problem lay with tenants' improper disposal of garbage. "I spend half my time cleaning up after them. They throw garbage out the window into the back alley and their kids steal the garbage can covers for sliding in the snow."

Version 3
Rat Bites Rising in City's "Zone of Death"

Rats bit eight-month-old Michael Burns five times yesterday as he napped in his crib. Burns is the latest victim of a rat epidemic plaguing inner-city neighborhoods labeled the "Zone of Death." Health officials say infant mortality rates in these neighborhoods approach those in many Third World countries. A Public Health Department spokesperson explained that federal and state cutbacks forced short-staffing at rat control and housing inspection programs. The result, noted Joaquin Nunez, MD, a pediatrician at Central Hospital, is a five-fold increase in rat bites. He added, "The irony is that Michael lives within walking distance of some of the world's best medical centers."

The stories share little beyond the fact that the child was bitten by rats. Each version is shaped or framed by layers of assumptions. To say each version of the story represents a different frame means that each has a distinct definition of the issue, of who is responsible, and of how the issue might be resolved.

Symbols carry the story line

One seldom encounters a news account that explicitly presents the core argument of the frame. More commonly, an image or set of images – metaphors, catchphrases, or anecdotes – carry the frame. Each rat story cultivates a battery of images.

Version 1 speaks of an infant left in his crib (read "abandoned") by a teenage mother who exercises questionable judgment because she is eager to cash a welfare check. Version 2 features a dispute and presents both sides – however, the landlord is given far more space to present images. He mentions spending "half his time" cleaning up after irresponsible tenants who throw garbage out windows while their children, petty thieves, steal garbage can covers. Version 3 uses comparative mortality rates, rat bite statistics, and respected figures like doctors and public officials to add an aura of scientific validity and further legitimate the frame. To save the story from sterility, Version 3 incorporates metaphors like "Zone of Death," and makes reference to infant mortality in Third World countries.

Implicit audiences

In choosing frames, news editors and/or writers are often implicitly speaking to and for definite audiences. Each version of the rat bite story might speak for and to a different audience. Version 1 might appeal to those who oppose welfare, or those whose worldview stresses individual accountability. Version 2 centers on a pluralist message, one that appeals to people who see society as a tug-of-war between interest groups ranging from tenant groups to free-market-oriented landlord associations. Version 3 stresses a public health ethic that would appeal to municipal health administrators, citizen action groups, and environmentalists.

Inequalities in access

All those who sponsor frames work to gain access to mainstream media. Even the dominant frame does not succeed without effort. Yet challengers who sponsor opposition frames must overcome the additional hurdles of inequalities in access, and a higher risk of frame distortion by the media. Those who support a dominant frame reap the benefits of media access.

Many are established institutions with well-staffed media relations operations. The Pentagon, for instance, has no fewer than 3,000 employees devoted to public relations, and publishes 1,203 periodicals. Each branch of the US military is also capable of launching an additional media blitz. Challengers can rarely match the resources of these dominant institutions.

Less access means the media and audiences have less familiarity with the challenger frames. And limited familiarity lessens credibility.

To combat anonymity, the challenger frame needs more access, more exposure than mainstream media usually allow. The dominant frame can call its whole argument to mind with the mere mention of symbolic elements; a challenger cannot rely on this easy familiarity. At least in the short run, time is on the side of the dominant frame.

Distortion of content

Dominant frames also have ideological inertia on their side. They build on assumptions so taken for granted that mainstream media perceive them as the only logical approach to a situation. Conversely, challengers present unknown information organized around unfamiliar political assumptions. The resulting frames initially seem strange, forced, or unnatural to the mainstream media and their audience.

One of the most common forms of distortion involves the presentation of challenger perspectives from within the logic of the dominant perspective. For example, in the 1980s, with government and big business declaring major and minor economic miracles, unions had an uphill battle to establish the validity of their complaints. Communities with high unemployment, particularly African-American and Latino communities, had to battle the dominant frame's contention: "There's work for those who want it."

Another common distortion is the flattening of challenger frames. Here the media's unfamiliarity with the challenger frame, coupled with the superficiality of US news formats, results in a weak version of the challenger frame. When a challenger frame is built on unfamiliar assumptions, the media will tend to translate the frame into the closest mainstream approximation.

Part of the problem is not what mainstream news includes but what it *omits*. Mainstream media pay little attention to history; the economic and political basis of an issue; or how events effect different groups of people in different ways.

Despite their disadvantages, challengers do often manage to gain a hearing for their opposition frames, albeit partial or distorted. Victory is seldom such that the challenger frame achieves equal status to the dominant frame. More commonly, the challenger frame simply does not allow the dominant frame to hold sway uncontested.

Activists respond with mobilizing frames

If an authority is acting in a normal, unexceptionable manner, the underlying dominant frame is taken for granted.

But frames are vulnerable. Sometimes actions or events occur that break the hegemony of the dominant frame. At these times activists need to offer an alternative frame, a mobilizing frame as a context for what is happening. Mobilizing frames usually have three characteristics:

- They define the issue, the responsibility, and the solution collectively.

- They are focused on conflict. There is a clearly defined opponent, "them," and a clearly identified challenger, "us."

- They launch a moral appeal. What's happening to the challenger is unjust, unfair, or just plain wrong. In some fashion it violates basic social standards.

Collective definition

A mobilizing frame pushes audiences to see problems not as individual but as collective. The definition of the issue stresses its social character and shows that responsibility for dealing with the issue is collective and that the solution happens on a structural level. Note that a demobilizing frame does the reverse, making problems ever more individual.

The rat bite stories offer an example. The most demobilizing frame is Version 1, which says the issue is teen mothers (who may represent a social group, but who are not organized and have few representative voices able to respond). Version 1 further says responsibility lies with individual mothers, in this case Angie Burns. Finally, as a solution, Version 1 proposes individual parent watchfulness.

Why is this demobilizing? Think of Angie Burns, a young, low-income woman struggling to be a good mother under multiple burdens. She has just been told that the rat bites are her fault. Is she likely to become more politically active? Does the solution suggested bring her into contact with other poor young parents who share her problem?

What about the other two frames? Version 2, the tenant-landlord frame, defines the issue collectively: the landlord versus the tenants as an organized group. The offered solution of Housing Court, however, may or may not be a collective one. Becoming involved in a public institution can, but does not necessarily, collectivize the solution. We would need to know if tenants' cases are being treated individually or collectively, if tenant organizers encourage tenants to appear en masse, to prepare collective testimony, to reach the public directly or via the media. A court-focused battle could instead revolve around individual settlements, which could isolate the tenants from each other.

The issue of collectivization also arises with the public health frame. Is Angie Burns offered any collective support by this frame? Or is she told that sympathetic city officials and state officials are pleading with federal officials on her behalf? The mobilization potential of the frame depends on whether or not community residents vulnerable to the rat epidemic are actively included in the solution. Thus the public health frame could mobilize, or it could drift into a defense of the modern social welfare state.

Conflict

The tenant-landlord frame focuses more than the others on conflict. It has two clearly drawn sides locked in battle over the issue at hand. The other two frames have an unclear target or an unclear challenger. Angie and mothers like her are the clear target of the first frame, but they are not considered a group, and they oppose no other group. Likewise, the public health frame does not draw clear sides. Public health officials closest to the scene generally see themselves as allied with the residents, yet the relation between local and federal public health agencies is one of cooperation as well as conflict. For the public health frame to include sufficient conflict, a challenger group representing community residents would have to contend with a clear target which, it could be argued, was genuinely responsible for the problem.

Moral appeal

Having defined the challengers as a collective in conflict with some other collective (usually an institution), it is critical for the mobilizing frame to use a moral appeal to argue that the dominant frame-holder is violating shared moral principles. In the rat story, two frames make strong moral appeals: the anti-welfare frame (which stresses the wrongness of babies having babies), and the public health frame (which stresses the fundamental injustice of a baby in a wealthy developed nation being mauled by rats). For the tenant-landlord frame to include a moral appeal, the tenants would have to seem more than an interested party feuding over facts. They would have to present clear evidence that Henry Brown is not a responsible landlord and that he is insensitive to his tenants' suffering.

Activists can be more effective if they pay attention to the potential energy of mobilizing frames. But they need to be careful. A mobilizing frame is not a superficial creation designed to woo audiences. A mobilizing frame is one part of the sweaty, often tedious detailed work of organizing – identifying which groups share what concerns, and whether or not they feel strongly enough to confront an identifiable foe. As such, a mobilizing frame is not a kind of media magic, but is an approach to organizing that, by strengthening one's base, strengthens one's hand with the media.

Appendix 4

How to Boost Community Participation

IN 1999 THE US LEAGUE OF WOMEN VOTERS published the results of a large study of community participation. Below are excerpts from *Working Together: Community Participation in America*. The full text of the study is available from the League of Women Voters and from their website at *www.lwv.org*. Organizations with paid staff will find the study's conclusions most useful.

In their hectic lives, people do not want community involvement to be another rigid commitment to juggle. Organizers can deal with concerns about time by allowing people to schedule activities at their convenience, work on volunteer activities from home, and work for an hour or two at a time, or by allowing them to get out of their commitment if they need to.

Among people who want to become more involved, easing time pressures is particularly important. For people who are not currently active but want to become more involved, the ability to work for an hour or two at a time is one option that would make them more likely to get involved in a community or voluntary activity. This same group of people feels the ability to work from home is an important thing to offer.

For people who are currently involved and want to increase their involvement, the ability to work for an hour or two at a time and the knowledge that they can get out of their commitment if they need to are particularly important. Being able to bring a spouse or friend along to the activity is also relatively important for this group.

Understanding how their work will benefit other people ranks at the top of the list of things that would make them more likely to get involved.

Given their busy schedules, people want reassurance that their work will make a difference and that their time will not be wasted. While potential volunteers say that getting a direct benefit for themselves or their family is relatively unimportant, they do want to know that their participation will have a beneficial impact overall. Organizers can address this concerns by explaining to people how their participation will benefit others or benefit the community.

In one-on-one interviews, activists said that one of the most important elements in successful recruitment was educating potential volunteers about the problems the organization seeks to address. Education shows people the seriousness of problems; and it gives them concrete ideas about things that need to be done. It makes them feel like *they* can do something about the problem because they know *what* needs to be done and *where* to go to get involved. For the activists, educating fishermen about oceanic issues, churchgoers about homelessness, urban residents about inadequate transportation, women about reproductive rights issues, and homeowners about the indirect benefits of walking trails were all critical to gaining support for and participation in their respective organizations.

Overcoming concerns about the group's credibility is also likely to increase participation. Organizers can allay questions about a group's credibility by providing specific information about the organization and how it intends to accomplish its goal. This finding dovetails with advice from several of the one-on-one interviews, in which respondents underscored the importance of sharing organizational history and successes with potential volunteers as a means of building trust and instilling confidence. Several respondents from diverse organizations mentioned the importance of a clear mission in attracting volunteers. People feel most comfortable about becoming involved in something when they understand the goal and – for older and more established organizations – when they know that the organization has a reputation for effectiveness.

Choice promotes comfort. Organizers can deal with fears about lacking proper skills, wasting time, and getting stuck by allowing volunteers to select their desired job from a list of tasks.

Locating and using local centers of community interaction is critical to generating support. Personal appeals made in comfortable, informal settings were among the most effective means of generating new involvement. Greenpeace organizer Niaz Dorry went to the docks and to bars to recruit fishermen. Susan Yolen of Planned Parenthood of Connecticut said that Planned Parenthood now recruits at rock concerts. Cindy Mitchell of the Parkways Foundation approached people involved in Chicago's cultural organizations who were previously uninvolved in parks issues for help with

Garfield Park, and then sponsored park garden walks to attract other, previously uninvolved people.

In focus groups, people described the places where they talked most frequently with other people. Many of these sites are centers of informal community interaction. Participants reported that they interact with their neighbors at local stores and laundromats as well as at their children's schools and sports games, churches, workplaces, and on their streets.

People respond to messages that emphasize the tangible difference people can make in their communities. The two strongest messages out of the survey were:

- People should take ownership of their communities, get involved, and make a difference.
- People should join together to make a practical, tangible difference in the lives of those that are most important to them – families, children, friends and neighbors.

Using politics as a motivation for community action is less likely to be effective. Disengaged people do not connect politics – what they see as making deals, endless campaigning, and empty promises – with community activity. There was little enthusiasm for using negative impressions of politicians and political institutions as a catalyst for community based action.

Issues related to children, including mentoring and coaching and education, are most likely to mobilize the untapped reservoir of volunteers. Both in the survey and in the focus groups, children's issues stood out as a potential catalyst for motivating involvement for all demographic groups. In the survey, a quarter of respondents revealed that children and youth was the issue that would most likely make them become involved with (not just contribute money to) a group or organization. In all, more than a third of respondents mentioned something related to youth, education, or schools.

The trebuchet team from the Mount Pleasant
Liberation Army holding a rotten projectile cabbage,
cantaloupe and melon. The MPLA aims at liberating
the Mount Pleasant neighborhood from the yearly
invasion of the Molson Indy.

Recommended Reading

General

Albert, Michael. *The Trajectory of Change: Activist strategies for social transformation.* Cambridge, MA: South End Press, 2002.

Bobo, Kim, Jackie Kendall, and Steve Max. *Organizing for Social Change: The Midwest Academy Manual for Activists.* Minneapolis: Seven Locks, 2001.

Borovoy, Alan. *Uncivil Obedience: The tactics and tales of a democratic agitator.* Toronto: Lester Publishing, 1991.

Chong, Dennis. *Collective Action and the Civil Rights Movement.* Chicago: University of Chicago Press, 1991.

Falconer, Tim. *Watchdogs and Gadflies: Activism from marginal to mainstream.* Toronto: Penguin, 2001.

Fisher, Roger and William Ury. *Getting to Yes: Negotiating agreement without giving in.* New York: Penguin, 1981.

Foreman, Dave and Bill Haywood. *EcoDefense: A field guide to monkey-wrenching.* Tucson: Ned Ludd Books, 1987.

Johnston, Kenneth. *Busting Bureaucracy: How to conquer your organization's worst enemy.* Homewood, IL: Business One Irwin, 1993.

Kaner, Sam. *A Facilitator's Guide to Participatory Decision-Making.* Gabriola Island, BC: New Society Publishers, 1996.

Kretzmann, John and John McKnight. *Building Communities from the Inside Out.* Evanston, IL: Center for Urban Affairs and Policy Research, Northwestern University, 1993.

Lappe, Frances Moore and Paul Martin Dubois. *The Quickening of America.* San Francisco: Jossey-Bass, 1994.

Peck, M. Scott. *The Different Drum: Community making and peace.* New York: Simon & Schuster, 1987.

Putnam, Robert. *Bowling Alone: The collapse and revival of American community.* New York: Simon & Schuster, 2000.

Sirolli, Ernesto. *Ripples from the Zambezi: Passion, entrepreneurship and the rebirth of local economies.* Gabriola Island, BC: New Society Publishers, 1999.

Yankelovich, Daniel. *The Magic of Dialogue: Transforming conflict into cooperation.* New York: Simon & Schuster, 1991.

On Organizing

Alinsky, Saul. *Rules for Radicals: A pragmatic primer for realistic radicals.* New York: Vintage Books, 1971.

Amer, Elizabeth. *Taking Action: Working for positive change in your community.* North Vancouver, BC: Self-Counsel Press, 1992.

Engwicht, David. *Reclaiming Our Cities and Towns: Better living with less traffic.* Gabriola Island, BC: New Society Publishers, 1993.

Kahn, Si. *Organizing: A Guide for Grassroots Leaders.* Washington: National Association of Social Workers Press, 1991.

Staples, Lee. *Roots to Power: A manual for grassroots organizing.* New York: Praeger, 1984.

Warren, Mark. *Dry Bones Rattling: Community building to revitalize American democracy.* Princeton: Princeton University Press, 2001.

On Work and Money

Dominguez, Joe and Vicki Robin. *Your Money or Your Life.* New York: Penguin, 1992.

Needleman, Jacob. *Money and the Meaning of Life.* New York: Doubleday, 1994.

On Government

Berry, Jeffrey, Kent Portney, and Ken Thomson. *The Rebirth of Urban Democracy.* Washington: The Brookings Institution, 1993.

Dahl, Robert. *On Democracy.* New Haven: Yale University Press, 1998.

Mathews, David. *Politics for People: Finding a responsible public voice.* Chicago: University of Illinois Press, 1994.

Osborne, David and Ted Gaebler. *Reinventing Government.* New York: Penguin, 1992.

Yankelovich, Daniel. *Coming to Public Judgment: Making democracy work in a complex world.* Syracuse: Syracuse University Press, 1991.

On Media Advocacy

Dale, Stephen. *McLuhan's Children: The Greenpeace message and the media.* Toronto: Between the Lines, 1996.

Harding, Tomas. *The Video Activist Handbook.* London and Chicago: Pluto Press, 1997.

Levine, Michael. *Guerrilla P.R.: How you can wage an effective publicity campaign without going broke.* New York: HarperCollins, 1993.

Rosen, Emanuel. *The Anatomy of Buzz: How to create word of mouth marketing.* New York: Doubleday, 2000.

Ryan, Charlotte. *Prime Time Activism: Media strategies for grassroots organizing.* Boston: South End Press, 1991.

Salzman, Jason. *Making the News: A guide for nonprofits and activists.* Boulder: Westview Press, 1998.

Wallach, Lawrence, Lori Dorfman, David Jernigan, and Makani Themba. *Media Advocacy and Public Health.* Newbury Park, CA: Sage Publications, 1993.

From Jean's Favorite Endangered Species Recipes, a web site featuring Canadian Prime Minister Jean Chretien.
The site targets Canada's Species at Risk Act, which is next to useless because it applies to only five percent of the country.
For graphic recipes visit www.newcity.ca/cookedspecies.

Index

CHARLES DOBSON'S BIOGRAPHY reflects a life-long commitment to troublemaking. In 1995 he published *The Citizens Handbook*, which is one of the best on-line organizing manuals available. For ten years he wrote ad parodies for *Adbusters* magazine. He is the founder of Better Notice, which provides media training for activist groups. He is also associate director of the New City Institute which conducts research on sustainable development, and public involvement. The only place he hardly creates any trouble at all is the Emily Carr Institute of Art & Design in Vancouver, B.C. where he teaches creative problem-solving, communication design, sociology and cultural literacy.

If you have enjoyed *The Troublemaker's Teaparty*,
you might also enjoy other

BOOKS TO BUILD A NEW SOCIETY

Our books provide positive solutions for people who want to
make a difference. We specialize in:

Sustainable Living • Ecological Design and Planning
Natural Building & Appropriate Technology • New Forestry
Environment and Justice • Conscientious Commerce
Progressive Leadership • Resistance and Community • Nonviolence
Educational and Parenting Resources

New Society Publishers

ENVIRONMENTAL BENEFITS STATEMENT

New Society Publishers has chosen to produce this book on New Leaf EcoBook
100, recycled paper made with 100% post consumer waste, processed chlorine
free, and old growth free.

For every 5,000 books printed, New Society saves the following resources:[1]

24	Trees
2,196	Pounds of Solid Waste
2,416	Gallons of Water
3,151	Kilowatt Hours of Electricity
3,992	Pounds of Greenhouse Gases
17	Pounds of HAPs, VOCs, and AOX Combined
6	Cubic Yards of Landfill Space

[1]Environmental benefits are calculated based on research done by the Environmental Defense Fund and
other members of the Paper Task Force who study the environmental impacts of the paper industry.
For more information on this environmental benefits statement, or to inquire about environmentally
friendly papers, please contact New Leaf Paper – info@newleafpaper.com Tel: 888 • 989 • 5323.

For a full list of NSP's titles, please call 1-800-567-6772 or check out our web site at:

www.newsociety.com

NEW SOCIETY PUBLISHERS